P9-CJZ-839

A Better Idea

A Better Idea

Redefining the Way Americans Work

Donald E. Petersen
AND John Hillkirk

Houghton Mifflin Company / Boston   1991

Riverside Community College
Library
4800 Magnolia Avenue
Riverside, California 92506

JUN   '92

Copyright © 1991 by Donald E. Petersen and John Hillkirk
All rights reserved

For information about permission to reproduce
selections from this book, write to Permissions,
Houghton Mifflin Company, 2 Park Street,
Boston, Massachusetts 02108.

Library of Congress Cataloging-in-Publication Data
A better idea : redefining the way Americans work /
Donald E. Petersen and John Hillkirk
    p. cm.
ISBN 0-395-58191-5
1. Industrial management — United States — Employee participation.
2. Work groups — United States. 3. Competition — United States.
4. Ford Motor Company — Management. I. Hillkirk, John. II. Title.
HD5660.U5P48 1991 91-26656
338.7'6292'0973 — DC20   CIP

Printed in the United States of America
BP 10 9 8 7 6 5 4 3 2 1

This book is dedicated to all those I've teamed with in common cause through the years, especially to my wife, Jody, cocaptain of the home team.

It is an old and a true maxim that a drop of honey catches more flies than a gallon of gall. So with men. If you would win a man to your cause, first convince him that you are his sincere friend. Therein is a drop of honey that catches his heart, which, say what he will, is the great high road to his reason, and which, once gained, you will find but little trouble in convincing his judgment of the justice of your cause, if indeed that cause really be a just one.

— Abraham Lincoln, speech in the Second Presbyterian Church, Springfield, Illinois, February 2, 1842

Acknowledgments

This book is not an autobiography. Nor is it a story about the Ford Motor Company. If it were, there is much that I would have to add, about the extraordinary efforts of Henry Ford II to provide the company with a stable management team and the strong support he gave us, the stability and continuity Phil Caldwell provided, and the outstanding job done by Harold ("Red") Poling and his management team. I would also like to thank numerous people who helped me prepare this book, including Nancy Badore, John Risk, and Ken Whipple.

My special thanks to John Hillkirk, with whom it was a pleasure to collaborate in writing this book, and to Houghton Mifflin for giving me the opportunity to have it published.

Contents

Introduction

If you look at the writings of various religions and of great leaders such as Abraham Lincoln and Martin Luther King, Jr., you'll see a common pattern of deep concern for people — and a desire to give them a chance to live meaningful lives. In business, we seem to lose sight of that, and to forget how much inherent potential each human being has. If given a sense of importance, a reason to take pride in their work, people will accomplish marvelous things. And they'll feel pretty good about themselves.

I'm writing this book to express my belief that business can and should be conducted in a better way than it has been in the past. We need to foster an attitude of trust, cooperation, and respect throughout our organizations. I certainly don't know all the answers, but during the 1980s, those of us at the Ford Motor Company developed a set of ideas and principles that helped to revitalize that company. Those ideas are what this book is about.

If Ford's managers had not developed a better relationship with the people inside our organization, the company would have had a difficult time competing in the 1980s. We would

not have developed the best-selling Ford Taurus, an affordable, stylish vehicle for today's middle-income family, or any
of our other huge successes, such as the 1990 Explorer. We
would not have out-earned General Motors for two consecu-
tive years, 1986 and 1987. We would not have moved from
last place to first place in quality among the Big Three automakers. And we definitely would not have gained seven
points of market share in an industry that has been so vig-
orously infiltrated by the Japanese. My experiences at Ford
convinced me that all U.S. companies — and, for that matter,
all organizations — can make tremendous quality improvements by tapping the power of teamwork: human beings at
all levels working together in a positive and nurturing environment.

By and large, most people want to do a good job, if given a
chance. Though everyone possesses a unique mixture of ten-
dencies, emotions, and attitudes, so that we're all something
like Dr. Jekyll and Mr. Hyde, our good motives usually out-
weigh the bad ones. If you can push the right "action"
buttons in people, most will respond with their Dr. Jekyll
side. I'm no psychologist, but I've seen that people definitely
feel better about their jobs when they have a positive frame of
mind than when they wallow in negativity.

These ideas didn't come to me overnight. They are the
product of forty years' experience. Just after I received my
master's in business administration from Stanford University
in 1949, I started working at the Ford Motor Company in the
product planning department. At the time, I didn't think I
would be at Ford very long. My wife, Jody, and I decided to
move to Detroit to see what things were like in the great big
East, and I was excited about playing a part in developing the
cars of the future. Still, I never dreamed I'd be at Ford four

decades later, let alone wind up running the company.

Over the years, I saw it all. Like everyone else, I had so-so bosses, SOB bosses, great bosses, and a wide array of relationships with coworkers. Some experiences were fun, and others were sheer drudgery. Early in my career, I worked in an extremely negative environment where people yelled at one another and bosses were very autocratic. I had a lot of trouble with this, and even considered quitting the company on several occasions.

Then, around the middle of my career, I was shifted to Ford's truck operations, as vice president and general manager. In my early days, truck was for people who were considered average, certainly not for fast-trackers. Trucks were definitely not the glamour end of the business, and still aren't; cars are. But in truck operations there was a high level of stability for employees, and trucks make a lot of money. I was surprised by how well everyone got along. I guess they had decided "Let's make a helluva good truck and enjoy ourselves while we're at it." The key people there had become a tight-knit team without the knowledge, let alone the urging, of the CEO or anybody else. That was a very refreshing experience. And it showed me what can happen when people work together.

After the truck experience, I had two more excellent assignments, first as the head of Ford's diversified products operation and then as the Detroit-based chief of international operations. Both jobs gave me a lot of autonomy, and I learned a lot about Ford's operations outside the United States.

In 1980 I became Ford's president and chief operating officer. That put me in a position to encourage more widely a spirit of working together, the way the people in truck operations did. Then, in the middle of the decade, I was elected chairman and CEO, a position I held until I retired in March 1990. The gains Ford made over those ten years were extremely exhilarating and rewarding, and they got a lot of attention. But personally, my greatest satisfaction came from watching people change the way they thought about their jobs and how they related to their coworkers.

This book identifies the philosophies and methods that can help any company or organization transform itself from a place where everybody hates to come to work to a place where people trust one another and enjoy working together. It presents ways to make the company as proactive and energized as it possibly can be, whether it's a manufacturing enterprise or a service firm. In fact, I would argue that a positive frame of mind is especially important in a service firm, where success hinges both on getting along with customers and on constantly generating new ideas. What matters most in a service firm is not what you do with your hands but what you do with your head.

The first part of this book, "The Transformation," walks you through a six-stage process that will help you get people to adopt these productive attitudes. The stages describe how you can make quality improvement your preeminent concern and suggest specific techniques — statistical process control, employee involvement, participative management, and worker empowerment — that should move you in the right direction. You'll learn how we launched the employee involvement program at Ford by helping hourly workers organize into teams, listening to their ideas, and giving them a real say in what was happening at the company. You'll also see how we trained thousands of managers to practice participative management, the fine art of listening to all ideas and points of view and giving all suggestions proper weight in the decision-making process. You'll discover ways of empowering workers and managers by pushing authority down, and how to reward team players instead of individualists.

There's one thing to keep in mind about the stages: changing a company's culture is a difficult and never-ending process. Almost every management book you read describes something sequential — "And then this happens. And then that happens." Yes, certain things do happen at certain times, but there is no reason to wait for one stage to end before you start another. At Ford, we recognized early on that we couldn't say, "First we'll improve the quality of our cars, then we'll tackle the relationship problems we have with our hourly employees." It all had to happen at the same time. We got so many things going at once that no one person could keep up with them. If I had tried to keep track of everything and had required everyone to report back to me at each step, we wouldn't have gotten anywhere. The process would have ground to a halt. That's true of most companies. The problems are too big, and too pervasive, to be attacked in a sequential fashion.

All the ideas you'll read about in this book should be launched whenever you believe you are ready to get started. Imagine, if you will, a volcano erupting, the lava slowly taking everything with it as it spreads in all directions. That's what happened at Ford.

Suppose you have Stage 1 through Stage 6 up and running. That's just the beginning. Employees are continually changing jobs; new people are constantly coming into the company, and all of them must be engrained with this positive way of thinking. In the second part of the book, "The New Philosophy," I describe what I believe makes a great leader and suggest you can spot such people in your organization. You'll see that a manager should also be a cheerleader, providing the positive reinforcement all of us crave and often deserve, especially in our work. You'll read about mining the talents and ideas that can be found in any group of people, whether in a business, a school, a government office, or any other organization. And you'll see why the word *quality* seems to be everywhere you look, and how you can empower workers to produce quality goods and services that can compete with the best in the world.

In the third part, "Pockets of Progress," I discuss the ways in which you can use these ideas to improve any organization, from a service operation in the United States to a manufacturing facility in Britain or Germany. As you'll see, these are fundamental principles, which can be applied by the military, by teachers and school administrators, and even by all of us in our daily lives. The final chapters of the book, contained in the fourth section, focus on my deep concerns about Japan and our nation's competitiveness, and contain some suggestions about what we have to do as a nation and as individuals to overcome our economic problems.

Now, let's get started.

The Transformation

1

Getting Started

Many American companies are in trouble, and I believe an important contributing factor has been neglect of the human element in business. For too long businesses and other enterprises have been managed with a top-down approach that leaves little room for the average individual to think. In the most autocratic environments, the chain of command works much as it traditionally has in the military. Only the leader and a few intimates and staff people are involved in developing a strategy and a plan of action. The leader gives direction; the subordinates obey. Employees have long since learned that their ideas are not wanted, so they simply wait to get "the word." They do exactly what they are told to do, nothing more.

The result is that only the mind of the leader, and possibly those of a few close associates, are involved in the creative and problem-solving processes. That small group may be very intelligent and experienced, but its members are not taking advantage of the insights and solutions that can come from people doing the actual work. Companies that are run this way are in serious jeopardy.

In most workplaces, the problem is not this glaring. The managers don't routinely berate or belittle people. They might even say they're interested in hearing their workers' ideas. But it's quite clear that most of the time, the leader's opinions are the only ones that really count.

Think about where you work. Does anyone ever ask you how things could be improved? Does your supervisor say he's listening to your ideas, but he really isn't? Are you encouraged one day, then criticized the next? In far too many cases, the supervisor behaves differently depending on the circumstances and how he feels that day. Much of the time he's friendly and considerate, perhaps even outwardly cooperative. Then suddenly he turns on you, criticizing you and undermining your confidence. In an uncertain environment like that, where people never know what to expect, they quickly learn to quit sticking their necks out and retreat back into their shells.

Operating like this causes enormous psychological damage. Basically, it erodes people's sense of self-esteem, making them feel that they're not worth much. It's hard to think of anything that you could do to hurt people much more than that. They begin to hate getting up in the morning. They still come to work, they follow the rules all day, and then they go home, tired and unhappy. Nothing changes in their work lives, and the old way of doing things never gets any better. Companies that operate this way become second-class. Sure, it's possible to hang on for a long time as a mediocre enterprise. There are plenty of them out there. But now we're seeing that more competitors, here and abroad, recognize that their workers are their greatest resource. They are using that vast pool of skills and knowledge to improve the quality of their products and their services dramatically. Companies that don't do so are in danger of being put out of business.

During most of my career, Ford used a typical top-down management approach. In the first few years after World War II, a vacuum in the management structure drew up the ladder many people who had been trained primarily by the U.S. military. This was true in many companies. Not surprisingly, a lot of emphasis was placed on management control and on giving orders, even though it was usually called giving direction. The result was that by and large, average employees concluded that they were being paid only to do what they were told. And though a lot of employees took initiative despite this atmosphere, too often people were reluctant to speak up.

In 1980, when I became Ford's president and chief operating officer, numerous people in many parts of the company were searching for a better way. Ford was operating in difficult times back then. In 1980 alone, it lost more than $1.5 billion — then the second highest one-year loss in U.S. corporate history. To make matters worse, our market share was slipping steadily, and customers were increasingly disenchanted with our cars. We were relying on the same basic design theme we had used throughout the 1970s, and we hadn't introduced anything dramatic in years.

The situation was so bleak that people in many of our organizations naturally started getting together to talk about what was happening. Talking was going on everywhere, more or less ad hoc. The discussions ranged widely, but what the conversations kept coming back to was "Why are we doing so badly? Why are our results so poor? What's wrong with us?"

Ford was rated lowest among the Big Three automakers in the quality and styling of its cars, and it was also pretty obvious by this time that the Japanese automakers had gained a substantial edge over us in the quality of their cars and the efficiency of their factories. We had to do something to regain our footing, to keep pace with the Japanese, and we could see that we had to get back to the basics of running a business well. But we honestly weren't at all sure that simply doing well what we had been doing would be enough.

In the middle of the turmoil, I watched an NBC documentary called "If Japan Can, Why Can't We?" It showed Japanese workers cooperating to solve problems on the assembly line rather than taking a break and waiting for the right specialist to come do the job. You could see that these people had a sense of common purpose and that they were working together in teams. They obviously were a lot more involved in running the factory than Ford's employees were.

The documentary also highlighted the role played in Japan's spectacular success by an American statistician and management consultant named Dr. W. Edwards Deming. The Japanese attributed much of what they had accomplished to Dr. Deming's influence. In the 1950s, he had taught them his managerial approach and his methods of statistical quality control. The Deming Prize for Quality Control is still the highest honor any Japanese company can receive; the awards ceremony is broadcast on national television.

That NBC documentary triggered me to invite Dr. Deming to visit Ford. He said he would come, but he insisted on meeting with me personally. That's standard procedure for Dr. Deming, because he believes that any serious effort to improve quality has to be supported by the top officers. The first time we met, he briefly described how his approach had been launched in Japan. He felt that the Japanese had applied his ideas successfully primarily because the nation's top fifty industrial people had listened to him and declared their support. He also reiterated to me that we wouldn't get anywhere at Ford unless the top executives were committed to making quality improvement our preeminent concern. Without that commitment, he said, our efforts would fail and there would be no purpose in his working with us.

Dr. Deming said he couldn't comprehend how I went about running such an enormous company, with almost 400,000 employees and facilities in nearly a hundred countries. He also told me how disappointed he was that he had never made any headway in the United States, because none of the top executives here supported him. Then he became a bit emotional and said, "Don, if you can make a real change in a huge company like Ford, you can have a major positive effect on this country."

He felt that we could make history. If Ford used his methods to make highly visible quality improvements with American workers, people would sit up and pay attention. He believed the ideas would catch on and snowball across the United States, just as they had in Japan.

I agreed with Dr. Deming's philosophy of management, and I especially liked the emphasis he placed on the importance of people. In fact, we hired him as a consultant, and I made a point of meeting with him myself roughly once a month. He usually had about three things he wanted to talk about. In the early days, he stressed the importance of applying statistical methods to achieve the desired improvement in quality. He warned me that a lot of people inside Ford would tell me that they knew all about it, that they were already using statistics. He then said, "Don, don't believe them. Ford is not applying statistical process control." Ford people might be using statistics here and there, he said, but not the way they should.

He was right. A group of young managers known as the

whiz kids had come into Ford after World War II and tried to put statistical process control into place. But it was the same old story: the effort was initiated by the people at the top; the employees in the plants didn't buy it and they didn't use it. They just papered their bulletin boards and office walls with graphs and charts of statistics that they could show to any management people who might stop by. But nobody believed in it. I suspect few actually understood the concepts. They didn't think it was necessary, and it just petered out. Dr. Deming convinced me that Ford had to adopt a disciplined approach to statistical process control throughout the company if we were going to recover. *Everybody* had to learn it and apply it on the job.

How does statistical process control work? First of all, you have to accept the fact that the quality of your products or services can only be as good as the system and equipment that produce them. When something's going wrong, 80 percent of the time there's something wrong with the way your production system or process is functioning. In a factory, the machinery and designs you're using may allow for too much variability — that is, they produce a good product one minute, a defective one the next. In a service business, a customer gets prompt and efficient service in one instance and gets left out in the cold the next — for instance, the mail arrives on time one day and gets lost the next.

To solve these problems, you have to dig into your manufacturing processes, or your service processes, and find out what's going wrong. The best way to do this is to teach your workers how to use statistical process control. Engineers, for example, can establish a range within which you'll have a satisfactory result. Statistics can alert you the minute you go outside that range, so that you know you've got a problem.

And you have to do something about it right then and there, when the problem occurs. Otherwise, at the end of the week you wind up with a lot of products that aren't any good.

Applying statistical process control takes discipline and training. But once your employees know how to use it and how to keep their own statistical charts and records, they can raise the alarm as soon as they see a problem arise. It's not a bad idea to give them the power to shut down the assembly line if they spot something wrong. What you're doing is letting your workers do the quality-control work previously done by a crew of quality-control inspectors. It takes a while, but most people will eventually see the benefit of using statistical tools. Yields get better, which means that there are fewer repairs to make and less material is spoiled. Things tend to fit together better and to get done on time. Eliminating the unnecessary work will lower your production costs — they can't help but go down without the inspections, the reports, and the surrounding bureaucracy. You'll find that many of your nonproduction people aren't necessary anymore.

Putting your employees in charge of quality will do wonders for their sense of self-esteem and pride in workmanship. They will see that your product or service is improving and will feel deservedly proud that they are the ones responsible. That's why, with Dr. Deming's guidance and support, we at Ford began to train our entire work force in the use of statistical process control.

At subsequent meetings, Dr. Deming began to talk about what he called the next priorities: primarily, the need to eliminate fear from the workplace and give workers the opportunity to do a better job. It all sounded so logical, because it seems to me that Dr. Deming's philosophy is rooted in basic concepts of human behavior, such as trusting your fellow man and living by the Golden Rule. Everything he says starts from the importance of the human being and moves on from there. Sometimes I think a lot of us get sidetracked because we believe that everything has to turn on a set of sophisticated or complex notions, but a seemingly simple humanistic philosophy is the wellspring of any transformation. Had it not been for Dr. Deming, I'm pretty sure we would have found a better way eventually, but it certainly would have taken longer.

Dr. Deming also led me to embrace the idea of continuous improvement. When we were talking in my office one day in 1981, he asked, "Do you want each of your employees to be better every year?" I told him that I did. And he said, "Then create a structure that encourages continuous improvement." In the past, our minds had been primarily focused on making substantial improvements whenever we started a new endeavor — constructed a new plant, developed a product, or installed a system or process. Dr. Deming helped me see why continuously improving is so important.

The real power of continuous improvement hit me when we were looking at the quality trends of American and Japanese cars from 1970 to 1980. The common wisdom is that American cars deteriorated badly in the 1970s. In fact they didn't; the quality was about the same at the end of the decade as it was at the beginning. But Japanese cars steadily improved year after year. The Japanese had opened a real lead on us in quality, because they understood that continuous improvement leads to lasting improvement. Major one-time improvements are rare. I was faced with the Japanese example every day, so it was seared into my brain. It's the same for anyone who has ever tried to diet to lose weight; you can see the drawbacks of losing twenty pounds one month, then backsliding the next, so you end up with a sawtooth pattern of improvement followed by deterioration. If you try that in a company for a decade, you get nowhere. But if you continuously improve, even modestly, the payoffs will be phenomenal.

At the time I met Dr. Deming and Ford started using him as a consultant, many other efforts to improve operations and solve problems were under way in the different organizations of the company. A variety of outside consultants were being used to address specific issues, visits were being made to other companies and to educational institutions, and a lot of internal get-togethers were being held. All of this was driven by a common understanding that incrementally improving the way we had done things in the past was simply not enough to get the job done. At many of our internal sessions, the questions most often asked were "What's our culture? What do we stand for?" People knew they worked for a company of great integrity and a lot of other virtues, but they couldn't put into simple and straightforward words a set of ideas that employees could understand and aspire to. Dr. Deming's philosophy, expressed in his "Fourteen Points on Management," the first of which is "Establish constancy of purpose," helped many of us zero in on some of the key concepts we wanted to express.

As an outgrowth of this process, Tom Page, Harold ("Red") Poling, and I, the top three operating people, volunteered to hold a series of meetings with a randomly chosen group of individuals from various organizations to see if we could put something on paper. It turned out that the group met quite a few times over a period of months. First we invited the group to write a proposed statement of Ford's values. Then Tom, Red, and I made suggestions. As the process continued, our thinking gradually came together. The real breakthrough occurred at a meeting when someone suggested that our values could be expressed with three *p*'s to make them easy to remember: people, products, and profits. The most important element was the sequence, with people first. When the three of us bought that idea and the group could see that we meant it, the rest of the statement was rapidly completed. Again, as in Dr. Deming's thinking, the emphasis was on people.

We then went on to develop a broad statement of the company's mission, its values, and its guiding principles. Although the statement wasn't approved as company doctrine until 1984, we were using it informally much earlier. The first principle — "Quality comes first" — also mirrors Dr. Deming's teachings. In fact, it became clear that improving quality was one goal we could all rally behind; if quality improvement was the focus of our efforts, everything else we wanted to achieve would follow.

As time went on and we thought more seriously about quality, we recognized that our definition was too superficial, too one-dimensional. It focused almost entirely on objective measurements of what was wrong instead of what was right in a car or truck. We weren't emphasizing in a concerted way the more subjective attributes, such as the look and feel that customers wanted to see in Ford products, nor were we specifically including these elements as a part of our definition of quality. It was another illustration that we were not being driven by what customers wanted.

I began to talk with colleagues about the need for a richer definition of quality. After a number of false starts at trying to articulate what was in my mind, I wrote a memo about the "driver's car," to develop the idea that the car and driver

Ford's Mission, Values, and Guiding Principles

MISSION: "... to improve continually our products and services to meet our customers' needs, allowing us to prosper as a business and to provide a reasonable return for our stockholders, the owners of our business."

VALUES: "How we accomplish our mission is as important as the mission itself. Fundamental to success for the company are three basic values":

• People — "Our people are the source of our strength. They provide our corporate intelligence and determine our reputation and vitality. Involvement and teamwork are our core human values."

• Products — "Our products are the end result of our efforts, and they should be the best in serving customers worldwide. As our products are viewed, so are we viewed."

• Profits — "Profits are the ultimate measure of how efficiently we provide customers with the best products for their needs. Profits are required to survive and grow."

GUIDING PRINCIPLES:

• "Quality comes first. To achieve customer satisfaction, the quality of our products and service must be our number-one priority.

• "Customers are the focus of everything we do. We must strive for excellence in everything we do: in our products, in their safety and value — and in our services, our human relations, our competitiveness, and our profitability.

• "Employee involvement is our way of life. We are a team. We must treat each other with trust and respect.

• "Dealers and suppliers are our partners. The company must maintain mutually beneficial relationships with dealers, suppliers, and our other business associates.

• "Integrity is never compromised. The conduct of our company worldwide must be pursued in a manner that is socially responsible and commands respect for its integrity and for its positive contributions to society. Our doors are open to men and women alike, without discrimination and without regard to ethnic origin or personal beliefs."

should be in perfect harmony when the car is in use. I tried to describe the way a customer should feel from the moment he or she opens the door. Everything needs to be well thought out, everything should be positioned just right, so that the driver feels as comfortable as possible. All the controls, all the dials, should be easy to locate, read, and operate. As the customer turns the key, the car should come alive, and it feel just right in use. I didn't write that memo to tell people specifically what to put in the car. I hoped to encourage them to be more conscious of these attributes as they designed and built the car and to keep asking themselves, "How will the final customer react to this? If I don't know, how can I find out?"

We also tried to instill the philosophy throughout the company that quality was everyone's job, not just up to the people in manufacturing. Basically, we said to people, "It's difficult to believe that we can have a truly excellent product unless literally every process and activity in the company emphasizes quality." This is a difficult concept for many to grasp at first, but the essential point is that each person, from the chairman of the board to the president on down, has an array of customers inside the company, and you need to find ways of fostering the idea that no matter what you do, you have to keep those customers in mind. In other words, you must constantly strive to do a better job for the people who receive the work you do, whether they are inside or outside the company. Every individual has to be convinced to strive for excellence in everything he or she does, even in minor details. If more and more people start thinking that way, everything within the whole system will get progressively better. And the company as a whole will continually improve.

We came to realize that the Japanese were already doing

this, and that was why they were beating us with the touch, feel, and sound of their automobiles. They paid extra attention to the quality of everything they did. Japan's Mazda, which is partially owned by Ford, helped prove the point. Mazda's Hiroshima plant was supplying automatic transmissions for some of our 1981 Ford Escorts. Here in our Batavia, Ohio, plant, Ford employees were building transmissions based on exactly the same design, but the performance of the two transmissions was dramatically different. The ones made in Japan were well liked by our customers; many of those from Ohio were not. Ours were more erratic; many shifted poorly through the gears, and customers said they didn't like the way they performed.

When we took the two transmissions apart, we could actually see a difference. The Mazda parts were beautifully manufactured and finished, and every measurement fell within very close tolerances. The Ford transmissions met the specifications, but there was a much wider variance in dimensions from one transmission to another. As a result, when the final products were assembled, they had more variance in performance. This showed us how far ahead of us the Japanese were in precision and control. They were operating within much narrower limits than the designs called for. The excellence of the workmanship on the individual components was remarkable. Discovering the benefit of this really prodded us along and helped convince us that we needed a definition of quality that included striving for excellence in every way we serve our internal customers.

Many people have the misconception that quality is the same thing as luxury. Dr. Deming helped make the point that even low-cost products can be superb and that quality is much more than just a product with expensive features.

That's something you have to keep in mind as you begin to redefine quality.

People frequently ask me, "What's the first step we should take?" As you can see from what we did at Ford, the main thing is to get started. Begin by talking about what's wrong and what the company should focus on. I would suggest that you make quality improvement your company or organization's number-one priority. You should also adopt the philosophy that people — not technology, not profits — are the key to your success.

Try to hire a good consultant who is knowledgeable in the application of statistical concepts to help you train your work force in statistical process control. If you can't afford a high-priced consultant, look for someone in higher education. Local universities and colleges are great resources. See if they have any experts in statistics who can teach statistical process control. Companies such as Ford, Motorola, Milliken, and Xerox, as well as the overseer of the Malcolm Baldrige National Quality Award, are also more than willing to point you in the right direction. In fact, companies that have won the Baldrige Award are required by the Commerce Department to share their quality improvement methods with other American organizations. But the most important thing you have to do is make sure everyone pays attention to the expert you bring in. I repeatedly made my support for Dr. Deming clear, and we held seminars so that two or three hundred people at a time could hear him speak.

I know we're living in tough economic times and people are hesitant to spend a buck to start a quality improvement program. But bad times are about as good an environment for change as you're ever going to get. Ford began its changes in the middle of some of its worst years, in economic terms.

People are deeply concerned during a crisis — and they're usually ready to try new approaches to preserve their jobs. You have to harness that energy and convince people to take a crack at making quality Job One.

Get started.

Stage 1: *Ideas for Action*

• Get people together and just start talking. Ask yourselves, "What do we stand for? And what is it we're trying to do?"

• Create a statement that outlines your company's mission, its values, and its guiding principles. Make quality improvement the organization's first priority. Put people ahead of products and profits on your list of company values.

• Teach your entire work force how to use statistical methods to improve the quality of your products and processes. Embrace the idea of making steady and continuous improvements.

• Broaden your definition of quality to include all the subjective attributes that surprise and delight customers. Urge employees to think quality in everything they do.

• Stress the importance of striving for excellence in serving internal customers. Urge employees to think quality in everything they do.

2

Showing You Mean Business

An organization's vision is worthless unless its employees understand it and are willing to help management carry it out. After your top managers have agreed that quality is the number-one priority, the next step is to look for ways to get everyone in the company to support your efforts. You have to create a sense of urgency that will dramatize what you're up against and convince everyone that important changes must be made in order to improve your quality.

The best place to start is with your disenchanted customers. Bring in groups of customers and ask them to explain in detail why they prefer your competitors' products or services. What do they like? Probe for as much detail as you can. Convince your employees that many customers prefer — maybe vastly prefer — your competitors' products or services.

In the early 1980s at Ford, we thought we were making some pretty good cars. Unfortunately, too many. customers disagreed with us. In Marin County, California, for instance, not one of the people in the focus group sessions I attended had any interest in Ford cars. In one session, not one owned a Ford or ever had owned a Ford. They scratched their heads, wondering if they'd ever been in a Ford. They thought Ford made a good truck but a mediocre car. Well, we videotaped those group meetings and brought the tape back to Detroit. Hearing people tear us apart like that was extremely sobering.

We also brought in a number of our best car dealers and asked them, "What do customers think of our products? What don't they like about them? Why?" We decided that we had to get out and see firsthand what our best competitors were doing. There was no mystery about whom we should study. We sent hundreds of people to Japan — a mixture of salaried and hourly employees — to visit Mazda, Toyota, and other topnotch companies. Just sending people out to visit competitors, even to another country, delivers a message throughout your company that you want new ideas. You're also giving your employees a taste of what the company is up against, which helps to sober them and to motivate them.

When we realized how efficient the Japanese were, we tried to figure out why. We saw how simple their record-keeping was and how all the parts and materials showed up just in time for assembly, which eliminated the need for elaborate inventory systems. For a while we thought these methods were limited to manufacturing, but eventually we realized that efficiency and simplicity are a part of every aspect of their companies. When Bud Marx, then vice president of finance at Ford of Europe, took a group over to look at Japanese financial activities, the group concluded that compared with the Japanese, Ford had far too many people working in finance. Having a top finance officer openly declare that his department was grossly inefficient was just remarkable; it sent shockwaves through the company.

In fact, I can't remember anyone who came back from

Japan thinking that we were ahead of the Japanese in efficiency. Before his trip to Japan, Bill Hayden, who ran Ford's manufacturing operations in Europe, was certain he ran the world's most efficient production operation. But he came back and openly admitted that the Japanese were far ahead of us and that their quality-control methods were demonstrably better. When someone like Hayden says that, things change. People realized that we had a real problem.

Before those visits, many of the people at Ford believed that the Japanese were succeeding because they used highly sophisticated machinery. Others thought their industry was orchestrated by Japan's government. The value of our visits, however, lay in Ford people's discovery that the real secret was how the people worked together — how the Japanese companies organized their people into teams, trained their workers with the skills they needed, and gave them the power to do their jobs properly. Somehow or other, they had managed to hold on to a fundamental simplicity of human enterprise, while we built layers of bureaucracy. This knowledge was essential, but the foremost importance of these trips was that people became convinced that changes had to be made.

You also have to take bold, highly visible steps that demonstrate the company's commitment to make quality improvement the number-one priority. Every management team that is trying to change a company's culture runs into skeptics who say, "Okay, you say that 'Quality is Job One.' But we're so financially driven and so cost-conscious, we'll believe you only when we see you putting quality ahead of cost." In order to overcome this kind of skepticism, the company has to prove that it will practice what it preaches. Every time your employees turn around, they should see management making decisions that will truly improve quality.

Through the years, Ford's management had closed manufacturing facilities as necessary to save money. Typically, the decision was a financial one that did not factor in the quality record of the plant or how the employees were working together. In the early 1980s, the company faced the choice of closing a fifty-year-old Norfolk, Virginia, assembly plant or a larger facility in Mahwah, New Jersey. Closing the Norfolk plant would have saved more money: it is a truck-only plant, far removed from any major markets and the rest of the truck operation. But the Norfolk plant was putting out quality products, and employee relationships were excellent. The Mahwah plant was relatively new, but the employees there weren't working together well, and their quality record was not good. Red Poling, who was in charge of Ford's North American operations, strongly desired to keep Norfolk open, because it was a plant in which quality was the top priority. To the surprise of many people, the company accepted Red's recommendation. This sent a simple message: from that day forward, the plants with the worst quality records would be the first to go.

We sent another message when the company was gearing up for the first Ford Escort. The Escort was a critically important new product — Ford's first front-wheel-drive automobile made in America. It was coming on the heels of the much-maligned Pinto. We desperately needed the Escort to prove that Ford could build fine automobiles, especially a fuel-efficient front-wheel-drive car. People were literally counting the days until we cranked up the plants and got the production lines flowing.

As launch day approached, the technical people in engineering and manufacturing knew there were still a lot of concerns. When Red flew down to the Escort plant in late 1980 to sign off on the car and approve it for production, he looked at the quality measurements, and he could see that the cars (usually a hundred are built in a test run) weren't up to par. In the old days, the decision made at the final sign-off meeting was pretty much *pro forma*. There was a final review, and then we started up. The assumption was that until corrected parts became available, we could eliminate the remaining concerns by reworking the units after they came off the assembly line.

Red wanted to show that we were operating under a new quality policy, so he got back on the plane and flew home without signing off on anything. "Let us know when you get this straightened out," he said. "We'll start production then, not before." So the entire Escort program was put on hold until the quality concerns were worked out.

If that weren't enough of a message about the Escort, Red also held up the production of the automatic transmission. In front-wheel-drive terms this component is called the automatic transaxle, and it's one feature you simply can't live without. The majority of American drivers insist on it, so it can't be held up. Right? Wrong. Red had heard that the transmissions were behaving erratically, so he decided to go to Ohio and drive some of the cars himself. His conclusion was that customers would not accept the level of quality he experienced. He held up production until the transmission was improved. That meant that the Escort started its life with just a manual shift.

As these stories about our commitment to quality started getting around the company, people began saying things like "Did you hear about that? They must really mean business."

We reinforced this with an action that affected the whole organization. Historically, employees in Ford plants were generally free to take vacations whenever they chose. While they were away, replacement workers, who simply could not produce products of the same quality as our full-time workers produced, were used to fill in. Red and I agreed to develop a plant-by-plant vacation shutdown pattern for all North American plants, under which all the hourly workers in each plant would take vacation at the same time, thereby eliminating the use of part-time replacement workers. Every year since — even in the boom years, when production couldn't keep up with demand — Ford has stayed with the vacation shutdown.

Beyond these highly visible actions, we began to put quality first on the agenda at all our major meetings. Even when we were losing money, we took time at the beginning of every meeting to discuss where we stood on quality. And everyone in the room, not just the quality manager, joined in the discussion.

That's what we did at Ford. You don't have to do exactly the same thing, but if your company is trying to accomplish major change, it helps you to get strong support if you can find some dramatic actions to take. Get out there and meet with your customers and study your competitors. It's going to take time and a lot of energy, but you'll be amazed by what you learn. Within your organization, find some ways to prove that you're not just paying lip service to quality. Look around for places where you can take bold actions to put quality ahead of cost. At that point, once you've convinced everyone that you're serious, you're in a good position to get all your employees involved in the effort.

Stage 2: Ideas for Action

• Look for ways to convince all your managers that your product's or service's quality must be improved.

• Start with disenchanted customers. Bring groups of customers into focus groups and ask them to explain in detail why they prefer your competitors' products or services.

• Visit competitors. See firsthand what they are doing better.

• Take bold, decisive actions to demonstrate that quality improvement is your number-one priority.

• Put quality first on the agenda at all your major meetings. Involve everyone in the room in the discussion, not just the quality manager.

3

The Power of Employee Involvement

The first step in revitalizing your work force is to launch an employee involvement program, as we did at Ford. If any company, of any size, hopes to make significant improvements, it has to take advantage of the know-how of everyone in the company, not just the people at the top. At Ford, we discovered that the best way to get ideas from all 370,000 employees was to encourage them to form what we called employee involvement teams, which met regularly to discuss ways to improve the workplace, the production process, and the lines of communication inside the company.

At Ford, our employee involvement program started slowly and had its ups and downs, but ultimately it was one of the driving forces behind the company's comeback in the 1980s. By late in the decade, easily two thirds of Ford's employees were participating in an employee involvement team of one kind or another. They contributed tens of thousands of highly worthwhile ideas, year in and year out. Without those ideas, the company's revitalization would have been impossible.

Working in teams is far better than trying to dream up ideas by yourself. A mental synergism starts occurring, and ideas rapidly bounce off one another. When a lot of disparate knowledge comes together, one person can pick up on what another says and add his or her insights; as a result, you get ideas and solutions that people working in isolation would never come up with on their own. In workplaces where there is no teamwork, ideas aren't exposed to many people. They're usually presented to one superior, and if that person doesn't like them, they're out the window. An awful lot of good ideas die that way.

Teamwork is also a great morale booster. We all have doubts. We all wonder how well we're doing in our jobs, and whether what we're doing will succeed. People need reinforcement, and teamwork provides that by putting them together with other workers who have similar goals, interests, and concerns. Each team can unite behind a single aim, which can be as simple as "How can we make this a better place to work?" or as lofty as "How can we combine our efforts to beat the Japanese?" An environment where people are working together instead of just for themselves also discourages internal rivalries and backstabbing, by keeping everyone concentrated on his or her own role as a part of a team.

The whole employee involvement process springs from asking all your workers the simple question "What do you think?" It involves the hearts and minds of your employees in everything you do, rather than merely saying, "Here's a set of actions for you to take. Just do them — you don't need to worry about whether they make sense to you."

Employee involvement should flow from the bottom up, not from the top down. It's no good for management to issue an order that says, "Starting next month, every employee will participate in a team meeting." It worries me to this day when I see a statement that says something like "Employee involvement is now working in seventy of Ford's plants." It's as if management has started counting something that employees were ordered to do and are now being scored on. People then start asking questions: "Okay, how many of your employees are involved? What percentage? And how often do they meet in teams? And why aren't they meeting more than that?" When you fall into that trap, you lose spontaneity and enthusiasm, and fear sets in. Your employees start saying among themselves, "Okay, guys, we've got to meet twice a week now instead of once. Management says so." They view employee involvement as one more thing they have to do, and the program loses its steam.

If managers can't order workers to form teams, what can they do? It is management's responsibility to put a framework in place that allows employee involvement to happen and to take actions that encourage workers to give it a try. At Ford, we looked out at our seventy plants and hundreds of offices scattered across the United States. We had more than four thousand people in some of those plants — they were the size of towns! We realized we couldn't launch our employee involvement program all at once, so we began slowly, developing what became an eight-step process. Obviously, not many companies are as big or as complex as Ford. Small companies, or firms that have relatively few facilities, should be able to launch an EI effort in every facility at once. The faster you get your teams up and running in as many places as you can, the faster your company will improve.

At this point, I'd like to offer a word of caution. The eight-step process I'm offering here is not a scientific formula. It's an outline, really, based on what we experienced at Ford.

There's nothing to memorize, nor any process to follow exactly. But these steps should help you to get an employee involvement program off the ground.

Step 1: Open up the books. You don't have to show people every nitty-gritty detail, but you do have to make employees privy to information that shows where you stand, what customers think of the products, and why you're asking for help. You've got to give your employees a taste of what your company is up against.

At Ford, the plant managers sat down with the union leaders and showed them some pretty sensitive financial data. For the first time, the managers shared information about the quality and profits at the individual plants. If we were all going to be involved in this together, we had to establish a sense of trust; we needed to cut down on the us-versus-them syndrome, which builds up walls between workers and management. Opening the books showed the union leaders that we wanted workers to be involved in the company's future, and it let them know precisely where we stood. Believe me, it was often a very sobering experience. Through the union leaders, we were telling our employees how the world really was. If they, as American workers, weren't willing to fight to improve the company, we could not compete effectively.

Step 2: Organize steering committees. Pull together a group of about ten people — half of them managers, half hourly employees — at each facility. Their responsibility is to oversee the employee involvement effort, keeping an eye on progress.

At each Ford plant, our steering committee was jointly chaired by the union leader and the plant manager.

Creating this committee sends a message that management is behind the effort. And putting hourly employees on the steering committee lets workers know they'll have a real say in the process. It's important to convince your employees that the effort is genuine, and that they shouldn't be afraid to join a team and speak freely about their concerns.

Step 3: Get outside or internal help. Employee involvement is a brand-new concept to a lot of people. You might want to find an expert, either inside the company or from a local university or college, who knows a lot about human behavior and how people relate to one another in teams. You don't need a sea of consultants; one or two should do the trick. With luck, you'll find experts who have had some kind of exposure to teamwork at another facility.

In addition to using Ed Deming, we brought in outside consultants (usually from small firms) to help the steering committees pinpoint problems they could attack. The steering committees met twice a month with the consultant or someone from Ford's industrial relations staff.

Step 4: Look for places to experiment. Don't worry about getting too scientific about it. If your company is large, select a handful of facilities as pilots. If it's small, you probably don't have much choice.

At Ford, we selected pilot projects at four assembly plants. At each plant, roughly two hundred volunteers formed problem-solving teams and went to work on just about any job-related problem they wanted to tackle. We also brought the local plant controller into the steering committee so that the financial side was involved as well. (It cost $200,000 per plant to kick off the employee involvement program. Most of that went to overtime pay in the first year.)

Step 5: Publicize your plans. Once you've selected a few pilots, spread the word to the local managers and workers that you're doing some experimenting and that it's neither a privilege nor a punishment to serve on one of the teams. It's a learning experience, something that should help workers enjoy their jobs. This will encourage people to volunteer when you decide to expand your EI program later on.

At Ford, we publicized the launch in union newsletters and on bulletin boards. As managers, we encouraged everyone to volunteer, but of course it was up to the employees to decide whether to take part.

Step 6: Launch the pilot. This is the most important step. Ask the steering committees you selected in Step 4 to pick two or three problem-solving teams per plant, then ask the teams to tackle something that is challenging but attainable. The problems the teams discuss at first should be relatively commonplace and easily understood by everyone involved.

A member of each team should act as a facilitator to help the team get started and to ensure that every member of the group — even the introvert — participates actively. Usually this person is outgoing, energetic, and a good worker. At Ford, a lot of women became facilitators. The facilitators can be trained by in-house experts, by consultants, or by professors at local community colleges.

Encourage the teams to begin meeting for at least one hour a week. But don't be surprised if they voluntarily meet a lot more often than that! Team discussions should be unstructured, and as agenda-free and paper-free as possible. Not writing everything down seems to prevent a bureaucracy from setting in. I remember years ago when everyone was talking about employee suggestion programs. Nobody met in teams; people just wrote suggestions down and put them in a suggestion box. Typically, the most junior people in management were given the assignment of responding to the suggestions. When I was just getting started, I remember, stacks of them were backed up on me. I certainly had little background or experience that would help me to judge the suggestions, and I remember thinking that the assignment was a chore, definitely not a stimulating, idea-generating experience. That approach has none of the dynamics of people meeting in teams and bouncing ideas off one another. (You also wind up with a lot of useless paper-shuffling.)

Step 7: Sit back and watch. Once the teams are up and running, the steering committees should see what works and what doesn't. Be careful not to keep score by tracking the number of suggestions made, the money saved, and so on. Comparing one team's success with another's can kill the free-spirited nature of the effort. You've got to be content with anecdotal and descriptive evidence that the program works. To see how things are going, a manager might want to sit in on a team meeting now and then and examine the mood of the group. Do the team members look forward to meeting together? Do they spend extra time discussing things? Or are they just going through the motions?

Don't expect dazzling quality improvements right off the bat. Early on, the teams won't come up with sophisticated ideas. Remember, you're launching these teams at the basic laborer level. The educational level may not be very high, and it will take awhile for people to get used to working in teams. At first this is a tentative, struggling process. Everyone needs to be encouraged to continue regardless of what they come up with. When we launched our program, I decided I would support the teams no matter what happened. I treated every idea as a meaningful success. These meetings aren't meant to produce miracles, after all; they are the introduction to a whole new way of working together. They are not an end in themselves; they are the beginning of establishing a new frame of mind. Through EI, you're trying to introduce people to the idea of taking the initiative and being proactive in everything they do — not just when they sit down at a team meeting to discuss specific problems.

Imagine that you are managing a professional baseball team that is racked by dissension. Players argue with one another, and everybody is out for himself. As the manager, you might encourage the team to hold some meetings when you're not around. The players might start talking and get things pointed in the right direction. But what's most important won't happen in the meetings themselves. The real pay-offs come out on the field, when the players are out doing their day-to-day jobs.

Step 8: Spread the word. Use your local experiments to let it be known that employee involvement works. Tell people what the teams have accomplished at the plants. Encourage managers, and union leaders if you have a union, to testify that it works. Better yet, have the employees who achieved the success tell their stories. It's much more credible, and people enjoy talking about their achievements time and time again.

At Ford, we asked our industrial relations people and the steering committee members to go from plant to plant to teach others what employee involvement had accomplished. As the program began to take off, the hourly workers still couldn't believe it was happening. Many thought, "Oh, my God, the management of the company actually came to the people doing the work and said, 'What could we do? And what should we do?' " As they heard more and more stories, a lot of them were convinced to give it a shot.

Of course, the adoption of employee involvement isn't going to be all smooth sailing in the first year or so. The only people who will actively participate will be the "early adopters," or natural experimenters, who belong to the portion of the population that is willing to give something new a try. But they are the ones you should count on to spread the idea to the rest of the employees. I remember asking Peter Drucker, the management expert, about teamwork and the need to foster a trusting and cooperative atmosphere. Drucker told me, "Don, if you can get a third of your people to buy in, that's all you need. The rest will follow." And he was right! The first third are your real leaders, and the other two thirds will join in after they overcome their skepticism. I found this was true not only with EI but in all our efforts to change.

How the Teams Work

You should begin by encouraging small groups of coworkers to organize into teams. Ideally, a team should have between six and twelve members. If you have fewer than six, you might not get a broad range of opinions, and a few personalities could wind up dominating the group. More than twelve members becomes too unwieldy, not to mention that it's often hard to get a word in edgewise.

The team's facilitator gets everybody together. If the boss is viewed as part of the team and wants to sit in, that's okay. But in my opinion, it's better if she doesn't. People need to feel they can speak freely, without any fear of retribution from the boss. The team might begin the discussion with a simple exercise. The facilitator could suggest, "Let's name ourselves. There's a name for this meeting and this group. What is it?" That might lead to a brief discussion about the company's or the plant's competitive position. "What are our quality problems here? Where does the company stand financially? What does quality mean to this group?" That leads to a process we call venting. Everyone in the group lets off steam, and begins to realize it's okay to speak out. Don't get all bogged down worrying about the topics; it doesn't matter what people are discussing. The important thing is to get everybody talking, and to make sure they all feel comfortable with one another.

The facilitator might ask, "What's bugging you? What do you cuss about in the course of a day?" As a team, the group can begin to discuss some real-life problems. "What could we do to improve the quality of the products we're making? Where are we throwing money down the drain?"

In the early stages at Ford, a lot of the problems the teams set out to tackle involved basic maintenance. "How can Joe work with water dripping on the back of his neck? What about all the sand in the paint, the dust in the air?" These may sound like simple problems, but they're not simple for Joe, who's standing there trying to work with water dripping on his neck all day long. Plus, what people talk about is getting rid of problems, and getting rid of problems means getting rid of rework and defects and all the hassles that hamper a worker's ability to do the job well. Yes, that benefits the employees, but it's also good for the company.

If a team isn't getting anywhere, it's probably because the facilitator hasn't been trained to lead discussions. Or the group doesn't have a facilitator at all. Two or three strong personalities are probably dominating the conversation. If that happens, I would suggest that someone say, "Let's get an idea from each of us. Let's just go around the table, and each person throw out a suggestion for improvement that we can talk about." That should quiet down the domineering per-sonalities and give the quieter people a chance to let their minds click into gear and join the conversation. Like me, a lot of quiet people tend to sit there, because they're not automatically comfortable speaking to a group. But once you free yourself from that trap and say something, it's a lot easier to chime in a second time, and a third time.

The facilitators, as well as management, should encourage the teams to consider a wide array of alternatives when trying to solve a problem or make a decision. Often people conducting brainstorming sessions tend to consider only a narrow set of options — either it's leather or it's vinyl for the car seats; either we do it this way or we do it that way. But you'll be amazed how many more choices are available if you get a group together and think everything through. It's hard sometimes to be highly creative, and to brainstorm in a vacuum. That's where teamwork brings great power. Often you need another person who knows about a new technology or a new way of doing things, someone who can say, "Well, if I could do this, would it give you a whole new way to approach the problem?"

Let's say you're trying to choose between materials of substantially different cost for making a small part. People participating in the discussion might say, "Are you for quality? Then use the expensive material. If you're trying to cut costs, choose the other. Do you want to spend a buck or don't you?" But what someone should say is "Wait a minute, let's back up here. Let's see if there isn't a different way altogether. Maybe we should think about redesigning the part. Will using the more expensive material save money in other ways?" That sort of thinking will lead you to explore all kinds of alternatives in a team environment.

Gradually, your employee involvement teams will offer some tangible ideas for improving your products and the productivity of the employees. Some of the suggestions will be simple improvements — adding a screw here, changing a trim design there — but others will be more lucrative. At Ford, some of the suggestions from employees resulted in tremendous quality improvements. Others saved the company anywhere from $100,000 to $700,000 a year.

The hourly workers who built the 1984 Ford Tempo and Mercury Topaz offered more than 650 suggestions, three quarters of which were adopted. At the Rawsonville plant in Michigan, the toolroom team recommended a complete rearrangement of the room where the workers keep their tools, jigs, and fixtures. They installed entirely new cabinets and drawers to keep track of everything. This small effort saved employees an estimated twelve minutes per day, which translated into annual savings of $130,000. At the Monroe stamping plant, also in Michigan, an EI group known as the energy team started talking one day about the tiny leaks in their compressed air tanks. After analyzing the situation, they used mathematics to determine that a one-eighth-inch hole would lose 730,000 cubic feet of air a month, at a cost of $119. That didn't sound like much at first, but they concluded that these leaks all over the plant cost the company $11,900 a month, or $142,800 a year! Repairing the leaks and shutting the tanks off at night saved Ford a significant amount of money. The team members now wear bright red jackets that say "The Energy Team." Their energy-saving crusade saved the company $1.2 million in 1990 alone.

Ford obviously benefitted from the employee involvement program, but many people were struck by the improvements in workers' morale. Roughly two years after the program began, the company and the United Auto Workers union asked 748 hourly workers how they felt about working at

Ford. About 82 percent said they were satisfied, whereas only 58 percent had said that before employee involvement got off the ground. Nancy Badore, one of the key players in launching the EI program, remembers what it was like: "Suddenly the people meeting in the teams were coming up with the same kinds of hands-on solutions they used to fix circuit breakers at their church or to get stalled cars running. They were spending far more than an hour a week tackling problems. They gave up their lunch hours. There were lots of occasions where people who had been laid off came in to work to give their presentations. Others stayed late, changed their shifts around, so they could stay and be part of the team."

Presenting Ideas to Management

An important part of employee involvement is how the team conveys its recommendations to the decision-maker or supervisor. Getting people involved in improving things runs right into a brick wall if you don't have supervisors who are prepared to listen and let their workers have a role in the decision-making process.

As an example of how this might work, let's say that Joe, on the assembly line, thinks he needs a $50,000 computer-operated lathe. He's not sure his boss will approve. Using his training in statistical process control, he begins to do research to prove that the lathe would benefit not only him but his section of the company. How would the lathe improve quality at his work station? Would its precision help the person who handles the part three steps down the assembly line? Because of his experience on an employee involvement team, Joe asks another team member, Susan, in finance, to determine how long it would take to amortize the $50,000 investment. Then Joe raises the idea at his regular team meeting, presents his evidence, and tries to gain the backing of the group.

The members of the team discuss Joe's idea. Bob, who works next to Joe, supports the idea by saying that this particular lathe would cut the parts they are producing much more accurately. And Sam, from the department down the hall, says he used the same lathe at another plant and got outstanding results. Susan shows the team a spread sheet that analyzes the financial benefits of the purchase over its anticipated lifetime.

The team agrees with Joe's suggestion to buy the lathe. Armed with all their evidence and anecdotal support, the team leader recommends the purchase to the supervisor. Only a tough old autocrat could say no!

In cases where the boss does say no to a team's suggestion, he must be prepared to explain his reasoning. Everyone should know what he decided and how he reached that decision. The boss must basically say, "Whether you agree with me or not, here's why I don't think we should adopt the idea your team came up with." That lessens the possibility that employees will be turned off by the process and never try anything again. Over time, people will understand that not everything they advocate will be adopted. They'll begin to think, "Okay, maybe my idea wasn't exactly what we decided to do, but we met as a team and discussed it and I had my say. The boss didn't buy it, but I understand his decision."

What if the boss repeatedly says no for no good reason? If I were the team leader, I'd pull him aside and try to reason with him. I'd say, "Nine times out of ten, we're just not getting anywhere with you. Are you going to try to cooperate with us or resist everything we are trying to do?" If that didn't work, I might try to get someone from another department to act as an objective mediator. This person wouldn't be formally trained as a mediator but would be someone whom everyone likes and respects. With luck, we'd make some headway then.

What happens if Joe's supervisor agrees to buy the lathe, but it turns out to be a mistake, because the lathe causes more problems than it solves? An honest mistake should never result in punishment for an individual or the team. You're apt to lose a lot of trust if you come down hard and apply penalties. Instead, employees should be encouraged to look for a way to use the mistake as a learning experience. The manager or team leader might suggest that the team do an autopsy and figure out what they overlooked. It may not be easy, and it might take some extra time. But the team will learn from it, and it will help them make a better decision next time around.

At first we didn't have a formal program at Ford to help managers respond to workers in the employee involvement groups. We eventually came up with a training program that teaches managers what became known as participative management, which I discuss in the next chapter. But even before that stage, the better managers realized, as most will, that their best results came from listening to the people actually doing the work. Good bosses will begin to understand that trusting team members doesn't make them weaklings. They will see that teamwork improves the quality of their decisions — and of the end result. In fact, other supervisors may start wondering how they got so smart all of a sudden.

Expanding Employee Involvement

One of my favorite stories from the early days of employee involvement at Ford is about a tiny parts depot in Richmond, California, where a few hourly workers persuaded the salaried people to stay home for a week. They wanted to show their bosses that they did indeed want to do a good job and that they could take over a lot of responsibility. The hourly employees ran the place like clockwork that week and set records for filling orders accurately and on time. We didn't have many examples of teamwork and worker empowerment back then, so I went there to congratulate them. Not surprisingly, I found a joshing, friendly atmosphere that was very conducive to working together in a positive way.

Though the gains made in Richmond were outstanding, they were limited to one location. You won't see universal improvements in quality until teams are working together throughout your organization. Otherwise, the benefits of a team in, say, Richmond, a team in Detroit, or a team somewhere else will be dampened or even wiped out. For instance, a group of designers in Department A might be working together and coming up with some great ideas, but if the engineers in Department B or the manufacturing people in Department C can't work with the designers' ideas, you're going to wind up with an inferior product.

That's why we made a dedicated effort at Ford to expand our employee involvement program from the factory floor to every facility in the company. We put the car designers together with the people making the car. We put the engineers together with the people selling the car. Working in diversified teams puts people with various skills and knowledge together in the same room, whereas they might not ever meet each other without the team approach. A marketing manager obviously looks at the world a lot differently from the way a technical whiz does, just as an engineer's got a different view from a stylist's.

In the technical end of the business, we encouraged engineers and manufacturing people to get together and discuss more sophisticated problems. Often a design engineer would take the lead in this area, traveling to one of the plants and pulling together a team of people — machinists, welders, assemblers, skilled tradespeople, or anyone else he wanted. He'd show them a design on the drawing board (these days I should say on the computer), and they'd talk about potential problems or toss out suggestions to improve the design.

As time goes on, such get-togethers come to be more impromptu, which touches on an extremely important point. You're trying to foster an environment, not lay out a set of operating instructions. And the atmosphere you want to create encourages a team here, a team there, all of them active at the same time, tackling lots of different problems. If you reach a point where everyone accepts teamwork as a philosophy, people will automatically go into any situation or project thinking, "Who can I bring together to discuss this? Where's the best place to do this? When?"

It won't be unusual for people to be members of a dozen teams at a time. In fact, the extremely creative problem-solvers will constantly be in demand to serve on teams. Some teams will last for years, and others will meet for a half-hour and never get together again. It's a dynamic, ever-changing process.

In some cases, teams will be formed with people outside your own company. One day when I was at Ford's Dearborn

engine plant, I talked to a fellow on the line, a middle-aged
black man. He was showing me the equipment he was responsible for, and I asked him how he liked it. "This is
wonderful, just beautiful," he said. He then told me that he
had been sent by his supervisor to the supplier that made the
machine tools he used. He explained that he had been asked
to look at the layout and design to see if he had any suggestions for improving the plan and making it easier for him to
do his job well. (I could see that he was proud of this story.)
When he got to the supplier's shop, he realized how little the
supplier knew about how he performed his job. For instance,
the supplier had no idea where he stood in relation to the
equipment, or that it was awkward for him to have the
controls on one side of a particular machine. He explained,
"It would really help to have this knob here, and if this could
be here . . ." The supplier made a lot of changes for him.
"That really helps me take care of this equipment and do my
job better," he told me proudly.

Getting Out to Kick the Teamwork Tires

As I've already said, top managers must constantly encourage
teamwork, and the best way to do that is to get out there and
spend time with employees. Your top people shouldn't just
randomly visit plants or departments in your organization,
though. They should pick places that have shown a commitment to the employee involvement process and that illustrate
what you're trying to accomplish. You want to hold these
people up as an example of what to do and what the benefits
are.

As president and then CEO at Ford, I saw it as my role to

praise people, stressing their importance and calling attention to success stories. I often asked other senior managers which of Ford's seventy plants they thought I should visit. Which employees would benefit from having me come in and acknowledge their good work? We tried to pick plants with good reputations or ones where the workers had tried something new.

At the plant, I'd shake hands with a whole raft of people and have a lot of photos taken. That doesn't seem very important, but it's time well spent. I always walked, if possible; you don't want people shooting pictures of you riding a golf cart through a plant. I would stop and talk with half a dozen people at a time. After we had exchanged the usual pleasantries, I would ask, "How do you like it here? Having any problems? Have you been trained yet in statistical process control? Are you part of an employee involvement team?" Then I'd just follow the conversation.

The most honest and forthcoming people were almost always the hourly workers. I'm not sure I know why. I think the stereotype of factory workers is that they are sort of depressed and grumpy. But at Ford a lot of talk goes on on the floor; there's a lot of give-and-take and kidding around. It might sound strange, but I found the factory workers much more relaxed than the salaried people and those in management. I think that's why a lot of them (though not all) were willing to talk frankly and openly with me.

Maybe the white-collar and management types tend to get all hung up on advancing their careers. They're so careful about what they say and who they say it to that it's much harder to have an informal, unstructured conversation with them. I remember that at some offices they would meet with me in the cafeteria. A dozen or so chairs would be lined up facing one in the front, for me. Their idea of informal was having me sit instead of stand.

The factory tours, when I got to talk with hourly workers, were among the most gratifying experiences I had as president. I remember running into a giant of a man at our Buffalo stamping plant. He looked me in the eye and said, "You know, I want to tell you one thing. I used to hate coming to work here. But lately I've been asked what I think, and that makes me feel like I'm somebody. I never thought the company saw me as a human being. Now I like to come to work." In Kansas City, one hourly worker in a plant told me how great the managers were, that they were changing things in an unbelievable way. That's about the highest praise any manager can get. When the average worker, the one who has been depressed and frustrated for so long, starts to feel good about his or her job, you know you're getting somewhere.

I also kept my eye out for plant managers who weren't supporting employee involvement. A couple of times it was painfully obvious to me that a manager was not behind the team effort at all. As we walked through the plant, I could tell he had given himself a crash course in his workers' first names. He knew a few of them, but most of them looked at him like he was crazy when he called out, "Hello, Harvey. How ya doin', Jack." It was clear to me that he didn't really know them, and that he didn't have contact with his workers every day. A plant manager, an office manager, or any business leader should be out walking around every day. The good managers will know every single person, even in a plant or office of 2,500 or more. That's their world, and it's no great feat to know everybody. It's easy to spot the good ones. More often than not, the workers in the plant are the first to speak. There's an easy familiarity, and each conversation sounds like a continuation of an earlier talk between the manager and the worker, which shows that there's a continuing relationship.

If I saw plant managers who obviously weren't part of the program, I never said anything at the time. Back in Detroit, I would suggest that the division chiefs might want to look into the situation. In several cases, the plant manager was changed within a few months. Moving a non–team player to another job sends a clear, strong signal that the company truly supports employee involvement as well as the people who are giving it a chance.

At some point in each of my visits, I would sit down with the plant's operating committee and union leaders and ask if they had gotten started on employee involvement and if the plant's managers were discussing things with the union people. Sometimes they would get these embarrassed looks on their faces and start apologizing for not doing so. "We know you want us to try to do all of this stuff, but we just haven't been able to get around to it," they'd say. When I asked if they got together at all, they would say, "Oh, yeah, every Monday." What do you talk about? "Quality. Troubles. Problems. How to change things. Sharing power." All the right things. "Forget the titles!" I'd tell them. "You're already doing it! Just keep doing what you're doing." Even if they didn't realize it, they were already creating a fertile climate for change.

If you've decided to give employee involvement a shot, let me leave you with one gentle warning: don't do it unless you're serious about making a permanent change. Your employees are going to like the new environment so much that there'll be no going back. I remember in 1983, when a handful of Ford's executives and union leaders got together for the dedication of the company's new education and training center. At that point we had three years of employee involvement under our belts, and our financial position was starting to improve. One of the local union chairmen stood up and said, "This entire effort has been fine, and lovey-dovey, and all that. We've started a new era of cooperation and all that. But once the company is making money, how do we know that management won't slip back and become the same old arrogant bosses that they've always been?"

The question wasn't directed to United Auto Workers President Doug Fraser, but he asked to respond. "I don't think this management team is going to revert to the old form. I'm now convinced that this is a legitimate change," he said. Then he paused. "Beyond that, I'm now convinced that the people in Ford Motor Company like the way the company is functioning today; they like the way they're being treated, and they simply won't permit the company to go back to its old way of functioning."

People who have tasted freedom just won't let you go back.

Stage 3: Ideas for Action

• Make a conscious effort to treat people well and to encourage employees' creativity, not stifle it. That's what employee involvement is all about.

• Introduce your employee involvement program gradually. Ford's eight-step process may help you get started.

• Open up the books. Share information about the company's financial position.

• Make the goal of employee involvement to improve quality, not to cut costs. Train workers in statistical process control.

• Find employee involvement efforts that work and make them models. Spread the word throughout the company.

• Get out and spend time with your employees. Encourage top managers to visit plants and check the progress of your employee involvement program.

4

The Art of Participative
Management

Once employee involvement started to spread in Ford's plants, our upper-level management people began to ask, "What's the management version of this? How do we respond to the EI-trained workers? What's next?" Nobody was quite sure what to do or where to go from there.

One of the places managers first started asking these questions was in Ford's diversified products operation. DPO, a $15 billion mini-conglomerate that supplies Ford with everything from glass and plaster to electronic components and windshield wipers, was under tremendous pressure to improve the quality of its products and services. Basically, the people there either had to find a way of meeting Japanese standards of quality and cost or their operation would be closed down. The managers at DPO knew they had to make huge improvements, and they had to make them fast.

That burden fell directly on the shoulders of the head of DPO, a man I think of as "Gentle Tom" Page. Tom is soft-spoken, wouldn't hurt a flea, and never criticizes anyone.

There isn't anything on God's earth that could make him behave in any other way. He's also very open to dramatic change, and he wants to encourage people to work together. Tom was familiar with the successes we were having with employee involvement at the various plants, so he gave Nancy Badore, who had helped launch the program, carte blanche to teach the basic EI concepts to the managers at DPO.

Nancy, who has a Ph.D. in industrial psychology, began her career at Ford in the foundry division — as basic a manufacturing operation as you could find. That's about the last place you'd ever expect her to have started, but she has such a lively curiosity about what makes people tick in an industrial setting that she was able to make a place for herself there. She loves to tackle questions like "Why are there so many problems in factories? Why are people treated the way they are? Can't we make major improvements in the way people relate and communicate?"

Nancy began her mission at DPO by organizing a task force to study other well-run companies. She wanted to find new approaches that could be put to work at Ford. The task force, made up of eight people from various departments at DPO, made a list of about forty truly outstanding U.S. companies and then narrowed it down to six firms—IBM, TRW, 3M, General Electric, Dana, and Hewlett-Packard — that were growing rapidly and practiced "people management." Dana, for example, had transformed itself in the mid-1960s from an old-line autocracy to a team-based corporation, and 3M was well known for its risk-taking and innovation. Both IBM and GE have been recognized for treating their employees well, even though they are enormous and have extremely complex structures.

The task force spent six months on the road, talking to

CEOs, middle managers, and factory workers. They also interviewed management experts such as Peter Drucker, who had helped numerous American firms change their culture, and Tom Peters, coauthor of *In Search of Excellence,* who cautioned that Ford's transformation wouldn't happen by accident and that it would take at least five years before people were convinced it wasn't a fad. The companies the task force visited had the following ten things in common.

1. Each firm circulated a statement of corporate goals and values, and its executives spent 50 to 80 percent of their time outside their offices, trying to communicate those ideas to their employees.

2. All six emphasized the importance of people and respect for every individual. They agreed that the skills and quality of their people were their only competitive advantage. Products or technology can be purchased, but usually don't help the company for long.

3. They substituted trust for strict rules and controls. When the task force met with Hewlett-Packard's CEO, John Young, one of the first things he said was "We trust our people."

4. Every firm made a big fuss about being customer-driven. IBM told the task force that there were very few ways an IBM employee could get fired, but one of them was keeping a customer waiting or letting a phone ring more than twice in a customer service center.

5. All six used teamwork, particularly multidepartmental teams, to develop cutting-edge products and services.

6. They tried to eliminate layers of management and to drive down authority. At one Dana plant, there were only three layers — the hourly workers, their bosses, and the plant manager.

7. The companies emphasized free, open, face-to-face communications. Hewlett-Packard calls this "management by wandering around."

8. Managers relied on peers — and occasionally on subordinates — to help evaluate other managers. Team players were promoted over individualists.

9. All six offered sophisticated training for managers as well as hourly employees.

10. Managers at the corporations made a habit of asking their people, "What do you think?"

More than anything else, the task force's study confirmed what many of us already believed, and helped to convince Tom Page and Nancy Badore to push ahead with teaching employee involvement to upper-level managers. Nancy and a team of her consultants created a seminar, which every upper-level manager in DPO, including plant managers and the executives who ran the various divisions, had to complete within one year. The seminar lasted three days and was followed by six weeks of experimentation and a two-day regrouping.

When Nancy first pitched the seminar idea to Dean Siddall, the head of DPO's glass division, he frowned and said, "Excuse me, you mean we'll be taking the same courses as my blue-collar people?" Nancy quickly responded, "No, sir! This is different. This is a participative management seminar!" I think this was the first time she'd called it that, but people began using the term from then on. Paul Banas, who oversaw the various plant managers, said that employee involvement and participative management were like two sides of the same coin, and we even had a company coin made to symbolize this.

In a sense, employee involvement does feed directly into participative management. More than anything else, PM is a mindset — a new way of tackling problems and making decisions. It doesn't mean you delegate all your responsibilities to those below you, and it doesn't mean you start taking a vote on everything. Nor does it change the structure or hierarchy of your organization. Participative management is simply a style of operating in which you give your peers and subordinates an opportunity to say what they think, and you include their ideas in the overall decision-making process.

As a participative manager, you will be a lot better off, because you will tap into the vast number of ideas found in your work force. Your decisions will not only be more solid, they'll be made faster, and with everyone involved, there's a greater chance they'll stick. People throughout your organization will understand why you decided what you did. A lot of people worry that participative management slows you down, because you wind up sitting around some room until the group reaches a consensus. That is not what I'm advocating at all. The decisions still must be made by one person — and always within a set period of time.

Each of our PM seminars began with a high-ranking executive such as Siddall talking about keeping the business afloat, the competition, and so on. Then various managers and division chiefs met in what we call max-mix groups, where we'd deliberately mix, say, the engineering manager from Tulsa with the Canadian personnel manager and the accounting supervisor from Detroit. That way nobody had to worry that some other manager from the same facility would repeat what he or she said when they all went back to work. People would admit that they were suspicious of this newfangled participative management, and even that they would rather be out playing golf or back home minding their own business. We encouraged them to ask questions, even if they thought their questions were stupid, and to challenge the executive who had kicked things off when he or she needed it.

The questions for the executive were presented by a group leader, not by individuals. That taught the division chiefs a lot about their own organizations, and about what their people didn't understand and needed to know more about. People within the groups really broadened one another's perspectives. The marketing manager learned a bit about engineering, and the engineer learned something about marketing. The seminar wasn't designed so people could discuss some abstract theory like "six important elements of effective communication." They just did it. Instead of talking about interdepartmental communication, they experienced it.

Everyone at the seminar was given the Myers-Briggs Test, a simple examination that's fun to take and illuminating. The test is based on theories developed by the Swiss psychologist Carl Jung in the 1920s, and is used to determine a person's personality traits through a hundred questions that determine how he or she reacts to certain situations. One multiple-choice question is "Would you rather work for someone who is (a) always kind, or (b) always fair?" Your answers determine whether you are extroverted or introverted (E or I), sensitive or intuitive (S or N), thinking or feeling (T or F), perceiving or judging (P or J). The letters are then combined — ESFP, for example — to describe personality types. After people took the test at the seminar, they wore badges that showed their four characteristics at all times.

From there, the participants began talking about people who are detail-oriented versus those who focus on the big picture, whether people look first at the subjective or the objective, and how people feel about closure and finality. That led them to discuss where they were likely to run into tension in their relationships.

The Myers-Briggs Test reminds you that everybody is different. In any room, fewer than a fourth of the people think as you do, arrive at decisions the way you do, or think about the big picture as you do. It's helpful to know how other people like to conduct a meeting or write a report. A lot of what we call poor communication stems from differences among individuals. One person expresses something one way, and another interprets it differently. For instance, a manager who likes to assemble a lot of information that she can analyze before making a decision might have trouble communicating with a more intuitive manager, who ignores most of the details and makes a choice based on his instincts and on past experience. But if they know they think differently, they can factor that in. Each of them can try to learn how the other thinks and can get closer to understanding the other's reasoning. This also helps managers prevent personality conflicts from flaring up when two people at different extremes are simply not communicating.

One of the benefits of the test is that it shows you how to recognize the difference between introverts and extroverts. This is important for managers, because even though everything might appear to be moving along fine, an introverted individual can be building up a head of steam and not doing anything about it. By his nature, he's reluctant to take somebody on. Then suddenly he'll explode, catching his coworkers and his manager totally by surprise. Or an introvert might walk into your office and slap her resignation on your desk. The Myers-Briggs Test helps sensitize managers to the various personality types among their work force.

Most managers are TJs (thinking and judging), extroverts who are prone to making sharp analytical decisions and telling their subordinates what to do. The test identified me as an introvert inclined to be intuitive and feeling (NF). I'm told that my personality type — the INFJ — is found in only one percent of the population. The Myers-Briggs people say that INFJs "listen well and are willing and able to consult and cooperate with others. . . . They value staff harmony and want an organization to run smoothly and pleasantly. . . . If they are subject to a hostile, unfriendly working condition or to constant criticism, they tend to lose confidence, become unhappy and immobilized, finally become physically ill."

The Myers-Briggs Test, and a very similar examination called the Birkmann Test, helped Red Poling and me surprise a lot of people inside and outside the company, who fully expected us not to get along as president and chairman, respectively. I suggested that Red and I share our test results with each other. I read about him, he read about me, and then we had a professional explain what kinds of things we'd have to watch out for — how we might misunderstand each other. We saw pretty clearly how different we were and that we'd better not forget it. I'm convinced it helped us work together extremely well, despite what people expected.

In the early 1980s, the company and the press were seething with speculation about who would be the next CEO. "Which man, Petersen or Poling, is going to win?" People assumed that after a choice was made, we'd never be able to work together, no matter which of us was in the top spot. They were aware that Red and I emphasized different things. They thought that I would be after them for not putting this or that and who knows what else into the product. Then Poling would be all over them for spending too much money.

If the two of us were at odds and were sending the company in different directions, it would never work. But not only did we work together well, we became even better friends. We became a team whose ability exceeded the sum of the parts.

Red is an outstanding manager. He eats up factual information, computes it, stores it, and then applies it to various actions. He concentrates on the numbers — charts, statistics, and so on — instead of on written material. He's less interested in someone else's interpretation of quantified material; he wants to develop his own interpretation and to spot inconsistencies that need to be explained. He can challenge the daylights out of people on facts and financial details. He's much better at that than I am.

Red tended to trust my judgment on decisions about unquantifiable matters, such as how far to go in styling or which features to include on a given model. He recognized that I had been working with automobiles for nearly forty years and had dealt with every personality you could find. I do know how to analyze the facts. I'm an engineer by training, and I can read all the statistics and tables. But I tend to leave the details to the people writing the reports so that I can pay more attention to the written material. Primarily, I like to get a sense of what the people involved are trying to do and why. That isn't easy in many corporations, because the written word gets completely sanitized and lifeless. That's why I prefer to meet with people and talk with them in person. Between the two of us, Red and I covered the waterfront pretty well.

Anyway, on day two of the PM seminar, managers took part in what we called the valentines exercise. They were grouped by function — all the engineers in one place and the personnel people in another, for instance — and given eleven sheets of paper, one for each function. Each group then wrote a short note, or valentine, to the other eleven functions, describing "things you do that make it difficult for us to do our job well." After the groups talked for an hour or so about the notes they'd received, the whole crowd gathered again to report what they'd learned. This opened lines of communication that had been closed for decades.

Ford, like many companies, has long been organized by function. If you're an engineer, you and everyone above you reports to the vice president of engineering, and so on. In any case, all the people within a given function form one hierarchy. We call this "chimneys of power." Before Ford's transformation, people in one chimney were given no encouragement to cooperate with people in another. An employee's salary and benefits were based solely on what he or she did in a particular function; no one gained any points for helping someone from another group.

Naturally, people stayed where they belonged, and at times there was practically a civil war going on among the different chimneys. For example, the designers would say, "If you were halfway decent engineers, you could make it the way we want it." The engineers would say, "If you were halfway decent designers, you'd give us something that we could build." With all this backbiting, our cars sometimes ended up the losers. And people were focused on fighting each other instead of on collectively battling the competition.

The valentines exercise helps break down the chimneys. It shows people what they've been doing to each other with divisional fighting. They see that they've been working toward narrow functional goals instead of a common goal. The exercise also helps convince people that it's in everybody's best interest to share the many different kinds of expertise within the company to produce a better product.

Day three of the seminar was spent talking about what the managers had learned and what problems they needed to overcome in order to start functioning in teams. They were all pretty sober by that point and realized that they had a lot of work to do back home. In the afternoon, we asked everyone to take on a project he or she could accomplish in six weeks, such as changing every meeting to a participative event or letting someone other than the finance people write the business plan.

When they came back six weeks later, it was easy to see how much they had learned from the experience. Some had bitten off more than they could chew; others hadn't done anything, and you could tell they had made something up the day before. But most had made some real progress. The rest of the regrouping session was spent diagnosing how well we were serving our customers and setting some goals for improving the quality of our cars over the next twelve months.

At the same time that we were getting these seminars up and running, a variety of management programs were taking place in other parts of the company. As we progressed, we concluded that we were headed toward improving communications among people in all the different divisions and that it was time to start a more organized educational effort for the top two thousand executives in the organization. I asked Tom Page, who had excellent relationships throughout Ford, and Nancy Badore to create a seminar specifically for the top executives as a way of taking participative management companywide.

Tom was just about to retire, but I asked him to do this before he left. He and Nancy came up with the Senior Executive Program, which started in 1985, after I became chairman and CEO. At each SEP seminar, fifty people from around the world — Americans, Brazilians, Australians, and Europeans — came together for a week and talked about what we were trying to achieve. It was good for people from other countries to see what was happening in the United States. I'm sure that before they came, some of them were thinking, "This team-building is fine for Americans, but it doesn't apply to us." We had to shake them out of that and convince them that participative management can be used anywhere.

We grouped the executives into seven-person study teams. Then we brought in a high-ranking officer to set the tone and offer a view from the top. We put them through many of the same exercises we used at the DPO seminars. At the end of those five-day sessions, whenever possible, Red or I talked with the group. "You're among the top two thousand people in Ford Motor Company," I told the participants. "You're our most important resource. You're the ones who have to change the environment back at your home office."

SEP brought our senior executives a lot closer to each other. They're friendlier now, and the people who work outside the United States feel more a part of the Ford team. For much of my career, people in Europe and the United States rarely communicated with each other, but because of the participative management programs, they now talk openly and share their knowledge, which is quite a refreshing change.

Any company that is attempting to change would be wise to put together a participative management seminar and require every manager to attend. It's important to get people away from their day-to-day jobs and arrange for them to spend a considerable amount of time together. A small enterprise without the resources to run these seminars in-house should look for a university or training center that offers such a program. For example, the University of Washington's graduate school of business teaches participative management techniques in its executive education program; most of the people who attend are from small companies.

Like employee involvement, participative management is an ongoing process. A couple of years after Ford's first Senior Executive Program cycle, we brought everybody back for a seminar we called SEP II. The follow-up program showed me that we were making some serious headway in changing people's attitudes. When I sat in on the SEP I seminars, the executives' suggestions typically centered on things they thought I should do as chairman to help the company. If *I* would hand out these orders, if *I* would issue these decrees, then all kinds of wonderful things would happen. By the time they came back for SEP II, something had changed, and they were talking nonstop about what *they* should be doing, asking me whether they were on the right track. We did everything we could to spur those internal efforts along.

Pushing Responsibility Down

At every large company, about ten officers usually make up the management team. At Ford, this group is called the Policy and Strategy Committee, and every component in the company — Ford of North America, Ford's international operations, the Financial Services Group — is represented. The committee members are among the most experienced people at Ford. They have a broad base of technical and managerial experience, and many of them have worked overseas.

When I joined the committee in 1975, as head of the diversified products operation, the atmosphere left a lot to be desired. Committee members spoke only about their own businesses, so if you were last on the agenda, you basically sat there until it was your turn to talk. For instance, if the man who ran the car operations was discussing some problem he was having with an upcoming product, I wasn't supposed to offer any suggestions, even though I had spent virtually all my working life in product development. The only exception would be if he was having a quality problem with one of *my* products. Then I'd be on the spot briefly to say what I was going to do about it. Imagine how stifling that kind of attitude was.

The way we changed the dynamics of the Policy and Strategy Committee pretty much followed the pattern of our efforts at the plant and operations levels. We just started making changes to encourage participation. For example, Red and I held back from expressing any personal opinions at the beginning of the discussions. Also, I made a point of telling the committee members that they should feel encouraged to speak up regardless of the subject. This was hard for them at first; they certainly hadn't had any practice. I often polled the members individually for comments and suggestions, in effect serving as the facilitator.

The top group of an organization meets to accomplish quite a variety of goals, ranging from a free exchange of ideas about strategies for the future to final decisions on major programs. The traditional venue for the committee meetings was the rather daunting board of directors' room. That was okay at decision time, but it seemed hard to get ideas flowing freely about new subjects, so we changed the meeting place. Breakfast meetings worked best. Occasionally we also met off-site with expanded groups, dressed in sweaters and slacks, to get an even broader base of discussion. As time went on, I think we had some of the most candid conversations in Ford's history.

In addition to talking about how we worked together, we began discussing ways in which we could push responsibility down to the lowest possible level and empower the lower-level management team. For example, if an engineer has the knowledge to make a decision, then let him make it; if a department chief knows the correct equipment for the job, she should be able to buy it. In most companies, too many upper-level managers make all the decisions. They waste a tremendous amount of time that way, because it means that the people doing the work are busy preparing detailed documents for the decision-makers to review instead of getting the job done. And as an idea gets passed up the pyramid, everybody who sees it tries to rewrite, redo, and reconceive it. In the meantime, a bunch of smart people are being paid to sit around waiting for somebody to tell them what to do. Having all decisions made at a higher level also takes a psychological toll on lower-level managers, because they lose their self-esteem. They don't feel trusted.

The best way to show them that you do trust them is to let them spend more money. In any organization, a manager's power is directly related to his or her authority to spend. When I'd have lunch with a group of lower-level managers and ask them what stopped them from making more decisions on their own, the response was almost always about money. Recognizing this, we asked our financial people to look for ways to delegate more spending authority to levels closer to where the work was done. They gathered a group of knowledgeable controllers and other financial officers and met regularly to review delegation of authority throughout the company. These reviews went on for many months, and major actions were taken as a result. Today Ford probably delegates more authority further down in the organization than any company of its size and magnitude of spending. This may sound like a scary move, but many spending authorities doubled or increased by many factors. Of course, we still kept strong overall financial controls in place. I suspect the review process continues today.

In some cases, we had to build up the status of a given group of managers. One example is the Technical Affairs Committee of the company, which is made up of the highest-ranking technical people and is therefore a powerful group. Through the years, the group had never been proactive, and its members had rarely exerted their combined abilities to take strong stands and make recommendations on technical matters. To help change this, I went to as many of their meetings as I could, first as president and then as chairman. My message to them was that they were by definition the best, most experienced technical people in the company, and for this reason the company badly needed them to take a more active role. Again, it was slow going for a while, but as they became convinced that we wanted to hear them loud and clear on technical issues, they grew strong, and today it is rare to have major disagreements on key technical judgments.

Another way of pushing authority down the hierarchy is to eliminate excess layers of management. Many companies are structured too vertically, with a few workers reporting to an immediate supervisor, who reports to a department head, who in turn reports to an office head, who reports to a vice president, and on up. You don't need all those layers. Doing without some of them will be good in any case, because it will force everyone to delegate more: with more people at each level now reporting to one person, that individual simply won't have time to make all the decisions. You also greatly reduce the chances for errors in communication as a subject is passed up the ladder. Fewer steps, fewer errors.

There is one thing you should bear in mind as you attempt to empower people through these approaches: managers who have worked hard to gain their rank and power are going to fight you. They're apt to say, "I know exactly what I'm doing. Why should I let someone else make decisions instead of me?" They might even refuse to let their subordinates make a decision without their approval. "Before you do that, check with me," they'll say. That phrase, "check with me," is one of the most damaging ones I know of, because it shows a real lack of trust. Managers who always want the final say use it a lot. But if the whole company begins accepting employee involvement and participative management, the holdouts are going to become more the exception than the rule. They'll either get lost along the way, or they'll eventually become convinced that PM is the way to go.

Rewarding Participative Managers

Peter Drucker says that the best way for a company to show its people what it values is with the promotions it makes. At Ford, a manager's ability to act as a team player and to treat people with trust and respect is highly valued. In my last ten years at the company, I tried to make those traits play a large role in how people were evaluated and promoted. It sends an important signal when people who possess these qualities are seen to be moving ahead. (Of course, an equally important message goes out when people who are the opposite don't seem to get anywhere.) Also, if promotions are viewed as sensible and logical, people tend to stop choosing up sides and looking for political ways to influence the decision. I have no illusions that you can completely eliminate maneuvering and playing favorites, but you can definitely work against these activities.

When it's time to evaluate managers, you should gather as much information as you can by talking to people. As Dr. Deming likes to say, you don't need a formal performance review to see who's a team player and who gets along with people. It'll be pretty obvious. Who puts team goals ahead of personal ones day in and day out? Who is always willing to sit down and discuss things with people from other departments? At the lower levels, especially, that kind of behavior always shines through.

I remember hearing from trainees that John Risk, the product manager of the Taurus program, stood out. Why? "He isn't always looking over our shoulders. . . . He never says a bad thing about anyone. . . . He has a lot of confidence in himself — and he shows his confidence in us." So there was John Risk, the highly visible manager of the Taurus program, whose trainees and peers were touting him as a team player. Believe me, that's the best praise you can get. The people beneath you and at your management level in an organization are in the best position to see how you behave on a daily basis. They know whether they can trust you and whether you listen to them.

In most cases, peers, and not superiors, ultimately determine which managers advance in their careers and which ones don't. A manager's success depends not only on the work subordinates do, but also on the cooperation and trust he establishes among his peers, like the manager next door or down the hall. Without good peer-level working relationships, things often fall apart. An autocratic manager, a schemer, or someone driven only by selfish instincts can do a pretty good job catering to people above him, toeing the company line, taking instructions from a boss, and so on. He might even get away with being a bastard to his subordinates. But a manager who doesn't deal openly with his peers and who isn't trusted is in trouble. His peers won't share information, and they won't want to work with him. Actually, they'll avoid him if possible. When this person's superiors sit down to discuss promotions, his name will come up, and someone will probably say, "Yeah, he's smart, he's got a lot of experience, and his results look good. But nobody wants to work with him, because he's divisive, selfish, and arrogant, and he can't be trusted. His results make him look like he's a hero; he really isn't." The last thing the boss will want to do is promote someone who is so disliked by his peers. You simply can't put someone in charge of talented people if they can't stand him. And you can't make him a key team member if the others don't want him. If you promote him, you could actually lose some employees and damage the future of your enterprise.

It's also important to see how managers are viewed by their subordinates. This is where employee surveys — similar to the surveys that university students use to rate their professors at the end of each course — can be a big help. Most employee surveys are confidential, so workers can say frankly how the manager treats them and whether he or she fosters a team atmosphere. That's important to consider.

Some firms, Ford included, are experimenting with step reviews, in which the superior two levels above you — your boss's boss — conducts your evaluation. Because this person has little direct interaction with you, he or she has to gather information by talking to your peers and subordinates. This type of evaluation is very much in line with the ideas behind participative management, because it encourages managers to develop the kinds of personnel relationships that will eventually reward them.

People who become participative managers can dramatically improve the morale in any workplace, and the rewards you get through new ideas, better communications, and smarter decision-making will rejuvenate the entire organization.

Stage 4: Ideas for Action

• Develop a seminar to teach the basic concepts of participative management. Ask every manager to complete a five-day seminar within one year. Use the Myers-Briggs Test or a similar technique, the valentines exercise, and other such exercises in the seminars.

• Bring seminar participants back in and make sure they've done something to improve the environment in their home office or facility. This is an ongoing, never-ending process.

• Find ways to hold frank, open discussions at your committee meetings. Set a friendly tone that invites discussion.

• Look for ways to push responsibility down and give more authority to the managers at the lowest possible level. Give managers at lower levels the authority to spend more money.

• Assume you have some excess layers of management and eliminate them.

• Incorporate the idea of teamwork into evaluations and decisions about promotions.

• Find ways to reward true team players. Evaluate managerial performance primarily by talking to each manager's peers and subordinates. The final results must be there, but pay close attention to how the manager achieved them.

5

Going for the Brass Ring

One good way of reinforcing the employee involvement, participative management, and teamwork programs you've been working on is to launch a project that will incorporate all of them. This is a good way to integrate EI with PM, and if it works — and it will — the project will serve as an example to get others to believe what you've been preaching.

The 1986 Ford Taurus shows what an organization can accomplish when it applies all the concepts that I've been writing about so far in this book. Developed from scratch, the Taurus became one of the American automotive industry's most spectacular successes of the 1980s. It was *Motor Trend's* Car of the Year and quickly became the top-selling car in the United States. It also epitomized the new Ford company.

As you read the next few pages, watch how the Taurus evolved as employees combined their suggestions and their expertise to give the final product the subjective look and feel of what I called the "driver's car." You will also see that the team focused very much on the customer and what he or she wanted. The Taurus actually got under way around 1980, when employee involvement, participative management, and multidepartmental teaming were just getting started at Ford. We didn't really set out to use these new approaches for the development of this particular car, but that's pretty much what happened. Six years later, when Taurus made its debut, the EI, PM, and teamwork programs had permeated the company. The Taurus project was a real test for these ideas. It showed what you can accomplish when you bring a team of talented people together and give them the freedom to do what they know is best.

As you may recall, we'd already decided that "quality comes first" and "customers are the focus of everything we do" at Ford. Those two concepts were uppermost in our minds when we began talking about the Taurus. We had to identify our customers, figure out what they wanted, and apply everything we learned to the development of the car.

Following the principles of participative management, we brought together people from all over the company to talk about what they thought we should do. In the past, the product planners would have dominated these discussions. But we made a point of bringing in the marketing people early so they could tell us what the market research showed. We talked extensively about customers and their needs, and about the fact that Ford is a bread-and-butter, mainstream automaker, and about how average American families are our most loyal customers.

We knew we wanted to build a car for people in the middle of the market, in order to stem the rapid defection of young people, who were now often buying Toyotas, Nissans, and Hondas. After studying the research, the team decided that we should develop a $15,000 sedan for young and middle-aged customers. The price was roughly $1,000 more than the Ford LTD, which the Taurus was replacing.

Once we had made a commitment to the specific physical and financial objectives for the Taurus, we turned the job over to the team. We asked Lew Veraldi to head the group, but we were careful not to tell him what to do and to let him make all the day-to-day decisions. A job like this must be in the hands of the professionals — the people who are most qualified to judge how far to risk going with a car and what to do to make it as appealing and reliable as possible. Engineers, for example, have great experience and technical knowledge; they know how to build an outstanding suspension system, a superb braking system, and so on. But if engineers have been forced for most of their careers to keep their best ideas to themselves, they tend to say, "What the hell," and build cars that none of them are proud of.

Fortunately, we'd been doing a variety of things to convince our professionals that we were serious about giving them more power. For instance, when I visited the design center in 1980 to update myself on the future models, Jack Telnack and a group of his designers toured the studios with me. Frankly, I was disappointed with what I saw. At the end of the tour, I asked them if they liked the new cars they were working on. (These included a 1983 Thunderbird.) After some hemming and hawing, they said that they didn't, and we talked about why. It had a lot to do with lists of restrictions — assumptions about what they could or could not do, based on past experience and a general sense of resignation. That's when I asked them if they would design a 1983 Thunderbird that they would be proud to drive and to park in their driveway.

That visit gave Jack and his colleagues the confidence to do what they wanted to do, and it helped him change the way the designers thought about their jobs. Remember what Ford cars looked like in the 1970s? They were pretty boxy and stodgy-looking. Well, it may be hard to believe, but our cars in the 1980s, including the Taurus and the Thunderbird, were designed by the same people who designed the cars of the 1970s, after they had developed a more positive frame of mind.

For the Taurus, Jack's team decided to continue with the more aerodynamic, smooth, rounded shape pioneered in the 1983 Thunderbird and increasingly found in European luxury cars. Switching to this new look wasn't easy, but it was a challenge the designers yearned for. For the body they worked with the engineers to make all the surfaces as flush as possible, so there were smooth transitions from the body to the bumpers and flush-mounted headlamps and door handles. The toughest part was figuring out how to make the window glass flush with the car's body, so the car would have the smooth shape and aerodynamic qualities of an airplane. Customers might not see the difference right away, but they would sense that something about the car was newer and sleeker and that with its design, Ford had tried hard to improve fuel economy.

While Jack's team worked on the exterior, Lew Veraldi began pulling together a team of twenty-five people from different departments to serve on the Taurus operating committee. This was really fantastic. When your designers, your product engineers, and your manufacturing engineers are able to have a give-and-take discussion, they can come up with a car that is not only attractive but incorporates the desired functional qualities and can be manufactured and assembled easily and correctly. If the marketing experts are an integral part of designing the characteristics meant to please customers, you end up with a very appealing car. The service managers told us what we could do to make the car easier to service, and repair personnel suggested cutting the car's panels in a way that would minimize damage in an accident. Overall, everybody had a much greater say in the development of the vehicle than they had had before.

With the Team Taurus project, we also made a point of not passing the baton from one person to the next, as we'd done in the past. The heart of Lew Veraldi's team stayed with the Taurus program from beginning to end. I believe the reason General Motors has a Corvette today is that one man, Zora Duntov, made that car his mission in life. Both Ford and GM started making sports cars in the mid-1950s, GM with its '54 Corvette and Ford with the '55 two-seater T-bird. The Corvette wasn't much of a sports car at first, and neither was our T-bird. Ford always had some new leader stepping in, along with whatever engineers happened to be available, but Duntov was there with the Corvette through thick and thin. That's how you develop a product with identity and character. Others may have influenced the Taurus project, but Lew and his original team stuck with his vision, providing the continuity needed to avoid developing a mediocre car.

Veraldi's team talked a lot about improving the car's interior and adding new features. They sent a memo to co-workers asking them what they would like to see in this new car, and ended up with an exhaustive list, which the designers eventually narrowed down to four hundred features. Then the team purchased fifty of the world's best midsize cars and tore them apart to see how every feature and component was designed and manufactured. This process, known as competitive benchmarking, lets you see every single detail of the cars, from the size of the door handles to the speed of the windshield wipers, so you can analyze which ones are the highest quality, or "best in class."

After months of research, the team gradually decided which features to include in the Taurus. Ultimately, they found a way to include 80 percent of those four hundred features in our car. The interior designers added a lot of simple creature comforts — things that weren't necessary for the car to run but that would surprise and delight customers, including a slide-out container for coins and beverages, a cargo net to hold groceries in the trunk, a picnic tray built into the tailgate of the station wagon, and oil dipsticks painted bright yellow so they would be easy to locate. These features didn't come cheap. In fact, they added more than $500 to the cost of producing the vehicle. This brings up the point that there is usually another indispensable person on the team, the finance person. Murray Reichenstein, Ford's controller of product development, energetically worked with others to find ways to offset such costs, which allowed the Taurus team to add features that cost more but gave customer-pleasing value to the car. Murray was open-minded enough to look beyond a rigid budget and help planners and engineers make the product they wanted more efficiently.

The Taurus's creature comforts touch on an important point. When you're developing a product or a service, you have to look beyond what the average customer says he wants to things that he doesn't even know he can have. He doesn't know he can have them because he hasn't seen or heard of them. Coming up with features like this is quite a challenge, but it's absolutely essential if you hope to stay ahead of the competition. If you deliver only what the customer wants at the moment, somebody else is going to blow you away with something that goes beyond your product or service in quality or innovation.

As the Taurus began to take shape on the drawing board,

efforts to improve the car reached far beyond Detroit to the manufacturing and assembly plants. The various divisions within Ford didn't automatically get the contracts to build the Taurus's components; they had to compete in contests, often against outside companies, to see who should make the four-cylinder engine, the six-cylinder engine, or the automatic transaxle, for example. In almost every one of those contests, a Ford division in the United States was pitted against a foreign manufacturer. The U.S. divisions relied heavily on employee involvement and team effort to win almost every contest. Their efforts were almost like storybook illustrations of what can be achieved when the people in an organization have a common purpose and desire to achieve something — in this case, to use the Taurus to recapture a big slice of the huge middle of the U.S. car market. And if that meant taking some business from the Japanese, so much the better.

A good example was Ford's transmission plant in Livonia, Michigan, which was in danger of going out of business in the early 1980s because it built only outdated rear-wheel-drive transmissions. The plant was up against Mazda to see who would build the Taurus's front-wheel-drive transmission. The workers at Livonia formed more than eighty employee involvement teams, and as their ideas were adopted by management, quality began to improve on existing transmissions. Almost immediately, errors dropped by 50 percent, which gave credibility to their quality commitments for the new design. They devised ways of upgrading existing equipment instead of buying all new machines, which saved the plant about $1 billion. On November 12, 1981, the company announced to a roaring crowd that the Livonia plant had beaten the Japanese bid and would build the Taurus transmission. Not only did Ford keep the production of those high-value components in the United States, but the Livonia workers could feel proud of and responsible for the car.

Before we started manufacturing the Taurus, we sent managers and engineers to the primary assembly plants in Chicago and Atlanta to ask the hourly workers for their suggestions. We even took plastic see-through prototypes of the car, so workers could see how their piece of the puzzle fit into the whole. Following the principles of employee involvement, management painstakingly examined every one of the workers' 1,401 suggestions. We either adopted them or explained to each person why his or her idea wasn't used. Ultimately, more than seven hundred employee suggestions found their way into the final design of the Taurus. Thanks to Ford's workers, the number of panels on the side of the car was reduced from fourteen to two, which lessened the chance of leaks and excessive noise. Employees came up with ways to fasten all interior moldings with one set of screws. In Atlanta, the hourly workers pointed out that the design of the Taurus's instrument panel made it difficult to install accurately, which meant there might be gaps or squeaks and rattles. They asked us to center the instrument panel or align it somehow so it would go in right where it should be every time. Using a special pin that automatically centered the panel, we got rid of that problem. All those little things added up: the number of cars needing rework at the assembly plants dropped from 10 percent to 1 percent. And as the car went into production, last-minute design changes that used to cost almost $150 million were down to only $35 million.

Just as we'd hoped, the news about Team Taurus spread throughout the company. Almost everybody wanted to be a part of it, and every time you turned around, someone else had joined the team. It was so popular that we even created jackets with "Team Taurus" written on the back, and we gave out more than a thousand of them.

The team element of the Taurus project was expanded to include Ford's suppliers. We held a series of meetings with key suppliers — we called the meetings "MSB: Must See Before" — in which we showed them how their contribution fit into the whole project. When suppliers know how their product will be used, they can better understand how to improve quality and provide parts that function within the overall design. For example, when we went to see our carpeting supplier, we showed him how, when the carpet was installed in the panels in the station wagon, the grain didn't look continuous. He figured out how to make all the carpet grain match up.

As launch day approached, I admit, I was concerned that we might have tried to do too much at once. There were a lot of advances in this car that had never been tried before, particularly associated with the aerodynamic design. I was scared to death about excessive wind noise, for example, or start-up problems with the new front-wheel-drive engine and transaxle. But the team was confident that the car was ready, so we went ahead. The 1986 Taurus certainly had some problems, but the sheer rightness of the car carried us. Customers loved it. Most important, the whole effort validated the benefits of great communication and teamwork. The Taurus project energized designers and engineers and laid the foundation for much better relationships between them. It also helped customers and dealers regain their confidence in Ford.

Ultimately, the way Taurus was produced became the model for a half-dozen major programs, including the wildly successful 1990 Ford Explorer. In fact, more teamwork went into the Explorer than into the Taurus. Again, Ford's recent experience with the all-new V-8 engine for the 1991 Lincoln Town Car proved that we were on the right track. Teams of hourly workers, designers, engineers, and suppliers were formed early to work on each major component of the engine. They all contributed to the design of both the product and the manufacturing process. No one discipline dominated. Ford's Romeo engine plant, which makes the engine, is also run strictly by teams. Instead of having traditional managers, each area is run by the team and a team manager. Team members learn to do eight or more jobs, and they rotate regularly. The Romeo plant is as close as Ford has come to leapfrogging the Japanese in the use of teamwork to make a product of unsurpassed quality.

As I said about employee involvement and participative management, the way to integrate all of these ideas is just to get started.

Going Beyond Taurus

As impressive as the Taurus program was, many people viewed it as a one-time event that we might never be able to repeat. One of the reasons it happened was that Lew Veraldi was a company officer and had the confidence and personality to convince those around him to buy in to his vision and to support what he and his team were trying to do. He was also fortunate in that everybody knew the company's future would be affected substantially by the success of this particular car. That gave the effort high visibility, and when the team needed help from different areas, it usually got it, even though Veraldi was asking people who did not report to him to spend their time and money to help out.

We could also see that the teamwork on the Taurus, although incomplete, had resulted in much more interaction among the functional groups early in the process and had continued throughout the years of development. A lot more work was performed simultaneously and thus more efficiently, which resulted in a significantly improved final product.

As the Taurus program entered the final phases, we talked about how we could incorporate the concepts we had used for that project in all product development programs and how we could go beyond them to achieve further improvements. We recognized that simply because we had successfully formed a team to develop the Taurus, we couldn't assume that other efforts like that would naturally fall into place. We wanted to find out how we could weave what had worked in the Taurus into the fabric of the company.

We also talked about ways in which the Taurus project fell short of what we needed to do in car development programs in the future. For instance, it took entirely too long and cost too much. As forceful as Veraldi was, he didn't have the authority to move people in and out of the Taurus team anytime he chose or to order changes in the basic design without first consulting other managers, and the people on his team usually didn't have permission to make changes or agree to tradeoffs without checking with their superiors. The Taurus effort also suffered because the team didn't have a central location, where engineers, designers, and other team members could work in unison. As a result of all this, the program took almost six years from start to finish. Japanese firms such as Toyota and Honda can develop a car with a new engine and transmission in about four years, spending significantly less money than we do on engineering, facilities, and tooling before the cars come out. We also experienced far too much trouble with the car in the first year or so.

Identifying Lew Veraldi and John Risk early on as leaders of the Taurus team had been a big plus, though. One of the first actions we subsequently took was to organize our product development effort so that team leaders would be clearly identified for each car and truck line. Perhaps because Ford of Europe is somewhat smaller and less complicated than Ford of North America, we actually got off the ground there first. The organization was changed so that an individual was given overall responsibility for each product line, and representatives from each function were selected for the team. Ford of Europe appointed program managers, who were like team leaders, from a variety of functions; for example, there was one leader from design, another leader from sales, one from engineering, and so on. This made it possible to select leaders from a wider pool of capable executives and sent a message that no one function was to dominate the process. An added advantage was that when a program manager returned to his or her original function after being a team leader, that person was much more likely to cooperate with other program managers.

Not much later, Ford of North America picked up on the idea of program managers for both cars and trucks. On both continents, this concept was also applied to major component programs, such as an all-new engine. At first progress was slow. Ideally, each team member would have a lot of authority, which would give the whole team enough power to make decisions without having to check with a superior, or even several superiors in the different functional groups. For instance, suppose a team is discussing ways to solve a space problem behind the instrument panel; frequently, it's difficult to accommodate all the components in such a limited space, a problem that comes up more often now that we are reducing size and weight for improved fuel economy. The team might come up with a solution that is within the overall vehicle budget but that would require a change in the design of the air-conditioning system, which would result in a cost increase there. If the member from the climate control function can decide by himself to incur the cost, the team can move on to the next order of business. No phone calls, no letters, no carefully written cost analyses. If he can't, the whole thing is put on hold until he can get an okay from his supervisors. Meanwhile, the team is waiting, losing time and often losing energy and enthusiasm. The spirit of cooperation and the interest in the final customer gets lost. When this example is multiplied by at least hundreds, as it is in many companies, you have a difficult problem.

Historically, career progress has been determined within the vertical chimneys, with performance reviews, salary increases, and bonuses all based on how well an employee does in his or her particular functional group. But with Taurus, and now with all vehicle and major component programs, Ford's program management is cutting across chimneys horizontally, bringing the functions together in a team environment. As a result, individual goals are taking a back seat to a unified effort to make a product that meets customers' needs and expectations.

As I was retiring in early 1990, I met with a group of program managers from both the car and the truck divisions to discuss how this process was working. Our conversations were sobering as well as encouraging. They confirmed that there were still plenty of problems but said that they were definitely making progress. They were optimistic that the extraordinary effort the company was making would pay enormous dividends.

In mid-1991 I talked with a program manager about the way things work today. He is running a twelve-member core team that is supported by about 350 people, all of whom are developing a new product that will be completed in about three and a half years. It will cost Ford about $1.5 billion, and the focus is on significantly improving the cars Ford has on the market now. The program manager reassured me that he and his teammates have far more freedom and authority than Veraldi's team had. For instance, he was able to hand-pick several members of his team, and he had the power to veto anyone he didn't want. And in a radical departure from the Taurus days, all the key people on the team work directly for him, full-time for the duration of the program, and not for their bosses in their regular departments.

Generally, people are evaluated — and given raises — by their bosses in the vertical chimneys. But it might be a good idea to turn that responsibility over to the horizontal teams. Then each program manager would evaluate all the people on his or her core team, and they in turn would evaluate hundreds of others who spend most of their time working on that program. Anyone who was evaluated that way would realize that the company was mighty serious about teamwork, and that an individual's success hinged on what he or she does to help the team develop a superior car.

The program manager I talked with and the core team have a great deal of freedom to spend their $1.5 billion budget however they want, as long as they don't exceed the total. The overall financial objectives will be set and approved by the board, but the group can then make tradeoffs without first checking with superiors. That's important, because the people on the team can make better decisions faster. Without that power, they always have a ready-made excuse if things don't work out well. They can say, "Well, we tried, but we weren't free to do what was right." When people don't have that excuse to fall back on, they tend to put more of themselves into what they're doing.

Another dramatic improvement is that all people working on the team will be housed together. For the first time ever, a marketing expert is working in the same office as the rest of the team. Eventually, more than 350 people will be brought in to design the car, build clay models, and come up with a prototype. Much of this will happen in a single location.

With everyone physically together, it will be much easier for the team to interact. "Simultaneous engineering," or designing the product at the same time that manufacturing, assembly engineering, and processing are being done, will enable each function to assist the others and will optimize the result. Sharing information immediately among the different functions should cut down on the endless changes that are usually made in products as they move through development. Far too often, people at each stage in the development process feel compelled to make all sorts of refinements and end up sending the product back for another design. They are well intended, but those good intentions cost a lot of money. I'm sure there are Ford suppliers who bank on increasing their profits when the company changes the specifications and reorders entirely new parts and supplies. Developing the car in one place should also cut down on that.

Implementing horizontal teams isn't easy, but I'm pleased that Ford is continuing to take steps to strengthen the process. It's difficult for managers in the vertical chimneys to let good employees go over to a horizontal team for several years or to let their employees make decisions they used to make themselves. But Ford, as well as other American firms, has to begin developing products faster and more efficiently to keep up to speed in the world market. If these organizations direct their energies and resources to horizontal teams, they will be taking a huge step in the right direction. In fact, that's the best move a company can make to ensure that its future products will be better made, more appealing, and more reasonably priced than the ones it has on the market today.

Stage 5: Ideas for Action

• As the different elements of your new philosophy begin to take hold and spread, find a product or service program in which you can bring all the elements to bear simultaneously.

• The key step is to form a team to get the job done. Involve all of the functional areas of your organization on the team.

• Give the team and the team leader as much authority as you can. The team leader should have maximum flexibility to make choices within an overall budget.

• Group the team members in one location if you possibly can.

• Be sure the team is customer-driven; seek ways in which you can surprise and delight your customers. Look ahead several years to what people might need or want when your product or service hits the market.

• Involve your suppliers and employees at the plant level as early as possible.

• Spread the team effort throughout the organization in a way that weaves it into the fabric of your entire system.

6

The Plateau and Beyond

You're probably thinking that you're at the point where you can sit back and relax. You've got your teams up and going, and your employees and managers are working well together and communicating ideas back and forth. The quality of your products and services has improved, and you see no reason why it won't keep improving. Well, now the tough work begins.

After we started our employee and management teamwork programs at Ford, we experienced about five years of tremendous progress. Then we hit a plateau. The rate of improvement of our cars slowed, and we began asking, "Why aren't we continuing to get better? Are we doing something wrong?" Our quality wasn't slipping, but the improvement had slowed to a crawl.

We came to the conclusion that as long as we continued using our old processes — the basic systems we used to do our work — we had probably gone as far as we could by tapping our employees' ideas and improving the way people worked together. This led to two initiatives: one, called Alpha, at the corporate level, and another, called Concept-to-

Customer, at the Ford of North America level. Ford of Europe initiated a similar effort. The emphasis in all these efforts was (and still is) on examining all of the many processes used in manufacturing cars and trucks and challenging every one of them. Is a given process even needed? Can it be simplified? Are better processes available that we can adopt? Are we taking steps in the right sequence? This is difficult, conceptual thinking, and it takes the best minds you have, but unless you make the effort to improve your processes, your well is going to run dry.

Around this time I had another meeting with Dr. Deming. When I told him about the work we had under way, he sat back in his chair and smiled. I could tell he was relieved that we had recognized that we'd gone as far as we could with EI, PM, and teamwork, because that meant he didn't have to face the challenge of convincing us of what we had to do to keep from stalling out. Dr. Deming may never have worked for a company, but from his years of experience as a consultant, he knew we would reach a point where our progress would slow down dramatically without significant process improvements.

What happened at Ford is likely to happen in any business that attempts to do the things I've discussed so far. You will very probably see significant paybacks, particularly rapid improvements in the quality of your products and services, over a period that might last anywhere from a few months to several years, depending on how big and complex your operations are and where you started. If you're already doing a pretty good job, your honeymoon won't last long, because you don't have far to go. If your quality is erratic, as Ford's was, you could improve for several years. At some point, however, your rate of improvement is going to slow down, and that's when you have to start re-examining the way your entire business operates — from the processes you use to how your factory or office is designed. Going on to this second level of transformation is much more complicated than spurring employee involvement or engineering teams. It's difficult, time-consuming, and less easily defined, but you have to do it if you want to move forward.

Where do you begin? Start with your old pros. Find the veterans in the company who really know how your system works. In a manufacturing setting, these people are probably your sharpest engineers; in service, they're your smartest department managers. Ask them to free their minds and start thinking about entirely new ways of doing things. Tell them to question the things about your business that have always seemed unquestionable. If employee involvement and participative management have truly permeated your company, people will already be in a frame of mind to do some real breakthrough thinking. In your favor, you should already have a group of people who are prepared to take the initiative and try totally new approaches.

Competitive benchmarking, which I described in the Team Taurus story, can also help you a lot. Be sure to send people from your company to visit topnotch firms that are similar to yours. Engineers and technically skilled managers can learn a great deal by visiting state-of-the-art manufacturing plants run by Ford, Hewlett-Packard, or IBM, for instance, and a customer service agent or insurance salesperson can benefit from observing the operations at L. L. Bean, Nordstrom, or Federal Express. Competitive benchmarking is more than just picking up tips, though. Everybody thinks in a different way, and corporate cultures vary widely. Letting your managers and technicians have contact with people in other companies who are also working on invigorating their businesses can stimulate new ideas and open up dialogues.

In addition, you should do a lot of intensive brainstorming. Get people to think about ways to simplify each process and make it more efficient. In doing this, you might even discover that some processes aren't necessary. An example of this occurs when a magazine hires a free-lancer to write an article. She types the information into her personal computer, prints it out, and mails it to the magazine, where a news assistant retypes the article into another computer. Not only does this process waste time and energy, it increases the chances that an error will be made, because every time someone handles the information or converts it into a different form, mistakes can creep in. Such a process can be simplified — and often is, these days — by transferring the information onto a floppy disk and sending it to the magazine or by transmitting the information directly from one computer to another over the telephone lines or via satellite.

If you are unable to locate the problem in a particular process, be sure to examine the early stages, which are often overlooked. Any number of things might have gone wrong long before you ever fired up the assembly lines. I remember talking to a veteran employee at our Wixom plant's paint shop. He and his coworkers were having problems with blisters and pits that formed on the large plastic piece that surrounded the grille and headlights on the Lincoln Town Car. They had to do a lot of refinishing and repainting, and often had to scrap the entire piece. This employee asked his supervisor if he could visit the supplier of the piece to see whether a change in the supplier's process could solve the problem. He told me how he met with the hourly people at the supplier's plant and described what was happening. By going through their process step by step together, they corrected it, at a substantial savings to Ford.

A good way to catch problems early is to set up checkpoints. No matter what business you're in, there are always key times in a process when you can step in and evaluate your progress to make sure everything is going all right. If something is incomplete, people are often hesitant to face up to the fact. Someone might say, "We don't need to stop the clock. Don't worry, we'll get it right. We think we can solve the problem in a few weeks, and we'll make up the time somehow." If you let that happen a lot, pretty soon you'll be holding meetings just to deal with all the fixes that are late. Also, you wind up trying to make corrections on the run, which can be a deadly problem. Let's say that the engines in your cars start vibrating after a couple of thousand miles of use. Correcting that sort of problem after the plant is up and running is expensive and difficult. The inexpensive approach is to make certain that everything works right before you start spending heavily on machinery and tools. You have to evaluate this at the design stage, when frequently all you are changing is information on a computer.

One of the most difficult ideas to grasp, but one of the most important ones after your progress seems to have leveled off, is continuous improvement. It's difficult to get a handle on, primarily because it sounds so open-ended and because even more than employee involvement and participative management, it's really a way of thinking and not a process. The Taurus can be used again as an example. After its debut in 1986, we could have sat back and said, "Hey, it worked. We can just ride our success." That would have killed us. We would have been settling on a plateau of our achievement, and we wouldn't have gotten anywhere beyond that point.

But because we accepted the idea of continuous improvement, we knew we could never stop trying to find ways of making the Taurus better. That was hard for us, because we had already put in every feature and innovation we could think of. Still, we had to look for more of those creature comforts or whatever, to keep customers coming back and to draw new ones in. It sounds never-ending because it is. But instead of looking at continuous improvement negatively, I prefer to see it as an incredible challenge. And with employee involvement and participative management in place, you should already be prepared to meet the challenge and to take your achievements on and on.

A word of encouragement: this stage is difficult, but remember that if you've reached it, you are already on the cutting edge. Only a few companies — Ford, Xerox, Motorola, Milliken, Hewlett-Packard — are making some headway at transforming themselves into team- and quality-oriented organizations, but even they have an awful lot left to do. As you progress further, it gets harder to find companies you can benchmark with, because you've become one of the pioneers. You have to rely on your own ingenuity to keep getting better. The companies that continue to come up with new ways of doing things will be enormously profitable and will be the leaders of the future.

Stage 6: Ideas for Action

• Look for signs that your rate of quality improvement is slowing down.

• As early as possible, examine your underlying processes. Decide what is necessary and how you can further improve or simplify each process.

• Ask your old pros, the best technical people or department managers in the company, to look for ways to do this.

• Remember that somewhere in the world, somebody has a better process than yours. Use competitive benchmarking to find those processes and learn from them.

• Establish checkpoints for monitoring your progress, and make sure everyone adheres to them. If the required work is not completed, stop the entire process until it is.

• Be the pioneers. Look for cutting-edge technologies to help you improve or even replace a process you currently use.

The New Philosophy

7

People Power

My ideas about dealing with people have been formed over a lifetime. I grew up in southern California and the Pacific Northwest. In Long Beach, California, we lived in a neighborhood with people from all sorts of ethnic and religious backgrounds. In fact, our family was in the minority. Many of my playmates were Hispanics and blacks. When we moved to Portland, Oregon, my horizon widened, and I was exposed to other ethnic groups, such as Asians and Italians. I learned not to worry about the differences in people and instead to appreciate them. My parents taught me through their behavior that everyone is equal, and they encouraged me to be friends with all of the children in the neighborhood. But as I grew older, I could see that my friends and their families were discriminated against. It was not something I understood. To me, they were just the people from my neighborhood and school.

I remember one disturbing incident when I was in high school. I had become good friends with a Japanese boy, and suddenly he and his family disappeared. This was just after the attack on Pearl Harbor, when everyone was suspicious of the Japanese and thought an invasion of the West Coast was imminent. My friend and his family had been taken to an internment camp in Hunt, Idaho. That made an enormous impression on me. I knew they had been treated badly simply because of their background. It reinforced my belief that everyone is the same, no matter where they come from or what the color of their skin is.

Although my own family didn't have much money when I was growing up, my parents always praised me, especially for what I accomplished at school, and my dad told me to stay in school as long as I wanted and not to worry about whether we could afford it. My parents had an enthusiastic outlook on life. I can't remember seeing my mother depressed, even in the latter part of her life, when my father developed serious respiratory problems and she became the sole breadwinner. She was totally positive in circumstances that could easily have made her give up and say, "Why did this have to happen to me?" She helped me appreciate the importance of maintaining a positive attitude, whatever happens to you in life.

I come from a good Lutheran family, and at confirmation age I took a full morning of instruction every Saturday for about a year. All the way through high school, I seriously considered becoming a Lutheran minister. In fact, I was all set to go to St. Olaf's College in Minnesota as a first step on that path when World War II started. My older brother, Pete, who was attending Oregon State University, enlisted in the navy's V-12 program and was transferred to the University of Colorado for training. I could see that I was also headed for the military, so I enrolled at Oregon State for a year and then signed up for the V-12 program too. The navy sent me to the University of Washington for my training, and when I graduated, I decided to take my commission in the Marine Corps.

I was never called to action, but this put an end to my plans to go into the ministry.

The lessons I learned in church stuck with me, however, as I moved on in life and became a businessman. I sense that many people believe that by its very nature business is out of sync with Judeo-Christian values — that there is a built-in contradiction between making sound business decisions and doing the right thing by your fellow man. I disagree completely. I believe that a lot of religious principles, such as "Do unto others as you would have them do unto you," should be applied universally in business. I've tried to live my professional life that way, and my religious background certainly had a lot to do with that.

Baptism by Fire

After I got my engineering degree at the University of Washington and an M.B.A. at Stanford, I joined the Ford Motor Company, in 1949, in a department that was later called product planning. I was introduced into an environment that was largely run by fear. Life inside the company was typically defined by some head honker of, say, the assembly operations, who would come to work, hat on his head, at 3:30 in the morning. That meant everyone who worked under him had to be there at 3:00. That kind of boss was absolutely dictatorial. And he was typical of the managers of that era. If you were big, had a deep voice, and could obviously lick anybody, you were on your way right to the top. If you dared to object to what these guys said, they would browbeat you into submission. After what I experienced in my early years, I'm surprised I was still at Ford forty years later.

After a short stint preparing what I now realize were rather superficial quality reports, I shifted over to the actual product planning work. The group I was part of reported to one of the so-called whiz kids. We were among the few college-educated people outside the finance staff, and many in the group were pretty arrogant about it. To them, everyone in the company except them was dumb. They were very ambitious, and so was everybody else. People throughout the company were openly competing for promotions and recognition. At one point, a man with a job similar to mine but on the truck side frequently stopped by my office to tell me about some brilliant thing he'd done that day, making sure I understood that it was something I should have done but had failed to do. The environment we worked in fostered that kind of behavior in people.

At one stage early in my career I became a kind of editor, because I could write reasonably well for an engineer; writing is a skill that not many engineers seem to have. For a year or two I rewrote probably every report before it went out of the product planning office. I often had such a tough time understanding the presentations I was supposed to redraft, because of the technical content and because of the way they were written, that I had to ask the engineers and other planners to explain in plain English what they were trying to say. That job put me in contact with every division of the company, exposing me to just about everything that was going on.

A virtue of my product planning job, then, was that it involved talking to people throughout the company, especially salespeople, engineers, and stylists, about what they thought we should do for Ford's cars of the future. If it's done right, product planning forces you to get people from all the different departments to work together on the development of a car. But a lot of people resented the product planners in those days, because we were seen as young hotshots who thought we knew it all. I had to find ways to work with people and get them to trust me not to hog all the credit if we achieved something. I had to convince them that I would speak for the team and not for myself. In essence, I was learning the things I would later try to do throughout the company.

The going was never easy. Every time I turned around, some autocratic boss seemed to be bullying people. I once wound up working for a non-Ford man who had been brought in from one of the failing car companies. His behavior was the epitome of how not to treat people: he cursed and castigated his employees in public and generally ordered everyone around. Jody and I had just adopted our daughter, Leslie, and were trying to adopt another child. (We succeeded; Donald Leonard joined the family a few months later.) It was a recession year, but I was convinced it was time to move on. I told Jody that I didn't want to work for a company that had room for someone like this man, and she gave me her strong support. When I told him I had decided to quit, he said that was fine with him. He went on to say that he had friends throughout corporate America, that basically he knew everyone everywhere. It was his way of warning me not to say anything bad about him or he'd make sure I wasn't able to get another job.

I went home and told Jody I had resigned, but then Bob McNamara, who was then in charge of all the vehicle divisions, called. Bob said he probably knew why I had quit, but he asked me to come in and talk about it. He never directly criticized my boss, but he pointed out that it can take time to correct things. He asked if I would be willing to take a "holding pattern" job in another division. I had no other job offers and no real plan, so I said yes.

Before long I was back in the mainstream of car planning, this time for the Ford division. I won't rehash the Mustang story, except to say that it is an early example of successful teamwork at Ford. Lee Iacocca, Don Frey, a supplier named Gil Richards (who ran the Budd Company at the time), Hans Matthias, Bert Andren, Gene Bordinat, Joe Oros, Jack Pendergast, Hal Sperlich, and I all played a role. Lee and Don were my bosses; Hal and I were the planners, Gene and Joe the designers, and Hans, Bert, and Jack the engineers. Gil, as a supplier, was independently trying to sell a similar idea to Lee. A little later the team expanded to include an outstanding group of marketing, advertising, and public relations people. I don't think Lee will mind if I say that Hal Sperlich, who worked for me, was the key person on the team, but the point is that a large team worked interactively on the Mustang, and we generated a level of enthusiasm that was electric. We actually were customer-driven. We had a lot of fun, and we respected the abilities of the others on the team.

During my first two decades at Ford, I seemed to have a different job every year and a half. In 1962 I finally had the job I wanted most: chief of product planning for all Ford cars. But I wasn't there long before Lee Iacocca bounced me over to the marketing department to broaden my experience.

Throughout these years, despite all the ups and downs, I made a point of not attaching myself to any one person. At Ford in those days, you got ahead by picking your "star," grabbing hold, and then hoping like crazy that he would make it to the top and take you with him. This, of course, led many people to undercut the other stars so the right one would go sparkling into the sky. But with all the other things I saw going wrong, I didn't want to be seen as an ally or protégé of any one person. I stayed as independent as I could, always assuming that I wasn't going to stay at Ford long anyway.

Going Off-Road at Truck

My first real chance to break away from the old regime came in 1971, when I was named vice president and general manager of the truck operation. I was following my good friend Hal Sperlich into this job. As I've said, Hal worked for me on the Mustang, so it seemed to me that my appointment to replace a former subordinate was a message that someone in upper-level management didn't have much use for me. The truck division was traditionally where they sent you if you weren't on the fast track. The car division was the glamour side of the business, and people who went to truck rarely switched back.

I was bothered by the down side of this move but knew many of the people in truck operations and liked them. Several of the engineers and other pros were there because their superiors had thought they lacked something in personality, or smarts, or who knows what. A lot of them had been working at truck for years and knew they were staying there. The atmosphere was positive, because these people had come to know one another well and had found they liked working on trucks. Their feeling was "We're the truckers. We know what we have to do, so let's be a team and do it right."

The chief engineer was a great guy named Bob Gaines. Bob was a very religious person in a quiet way, and he was far up in the hierarchy of his church. He really believed in the Golden Rule and in trusting people, and in his own way he applied this faith to the philosophy at truck. Bob Gaines set an example and saw to it that everyone behaved like a trucker. Everybody admired him, even loved him, and the atmosphere he created for the engineers played a large role in what we accomplished.

In my four years in the truck division, I discovered that any organization can function better if people work together with a common goal of serving the customer by improving the product instead of playing political games. The truckers didn't call what they were practicing employee involvement and participative management, but boy, were they ever doing it! Anytime we had something to discuss or a problem to solve, eight to twelve of us would get together in my office or some conference room and throw everything open. People were much more relaxed than people in the car division, and nobody was afraid to speak up. People from finance, planning, manufacturing, engineering, and sales were sitting in the same room. When an issue was on the table and you had something to contribute, it didn't matter what role you were in; you spoke up, and everyone was interested in what you had to say. If someone from the car operation had walked in on one of these discussions, he would have been amazed.

All the systems and processes at truck were built around finding ways to get people to work together. Relationships were outstanding — you never saw product planners, for instance, treating engineers as anything other than the knowledgeable experts they were. No one got on his high horse and started dictating.

Whenever we went on trips to see how our trucks measured up against the competition's, we had a ball. My wife teased me by saying we were a bunch of grown men playing with our life-size Tonka Toys. Being out there on the road sometimes for weeks at a time, riding around, joshing and kidding each other, built a strong sense of kinship and common purpose. For all the fun we had, we were always focused on finding ways to improve our product, not to advance our own careers.

As a payoff for all this teamwork, we had a first-rate truck that customers liked and admired. In fact, around that time the difference in quality between Ford cars and Ford trucks was so great that customers began thinking of us as two totally different companies: car and truck. When our market share for cars was tumbling below 20 percent in the early 1980s, our market share for trucks stayed above 30 percent, right through the worst period. Many Ford dealers made it through the bleakest economic periods because of their sales of trucks.

As much as I enjoyed working in the truck division, my career seemed to be at a standstill. I was fifty years old; I wasn't getting any salary boosts or significant cash bonuses, and I was being passed over on stock options. It seemed like a logical time to leave and perhaps start thinking about a second career. I think I would have left the company if an opportunity that was presented to me in 1973 had worked out. A college classmate asked me to help him expand his family's company in California, but in the end his brother wasn't in favor of the expansion plans, so the offer never really got off the ground.

Shortly after that, Bob Hampson became the head of North American operations, which oversaw truck operations. In some way or other, Bob rehabilitated me at Ford. In any event, when they needed someone to run diversified products operations in 1975, they decided to gamble on me.

The Value of Teamwork

My years at Ford, particularly in the truck division, convinced me that teamwork is where you have to start if you want to revitalize a company that is infected with internal power struggles and individualism and has consequently become sluggish and unproductive. It's a matter of recognizing that your people are your strength and finding a way of helping them to be their best. Which do you think will give you the best results, some superstar calling all the shots or a group that combines its strengths for the good of the team?

Ed Deming's favorite example is the symphony orchestra, in which a collection of extraordinarily talented musicians forgo their own needs for recognition in order to give an outstanding performance. The smartest (and often best) athletes, such as basketball stars Magic Johnson of the Los Angeles Lakers and Isiah Thomas of the Detroit Pistons, are undoubtedly tempted to build up their own statistics at the expense of the team. But the Lakers and the Pistons would never have won a championship if Magic and Isiah had gone out there only for themselves. Each of them recognizes that in the long run, the team's success attracts more fans, which translates into more TV money and higher ticket sales. When that happens, the team's stars benefit the most.

The same is true in business. If your company does well, all the employees keep their jobs and get progressively higher raises. It's important that everyone share the financial rewards, not just the higher-ups. I'm a big fan of profit-sharing. A company is about a lot of things other than making money, but that is the primary purpose. When everyone contributes to its success, everyone should get a part of the spoils.

Not all your employees will believe in the rewards of teamwork. A lot of people pay lip service to it, but they're really only interested in themselves. This is most evident when times get tough. Whatever notions of teamwork were around go right out the window, and everybody starts heading off in his or her own direction. That's when you find out the truth about whether people are thinking about "we" and "us" or just about "you" and "me."

I think companies can overcome this problem. One of the best ways is to find team leaders at every level and help them set an example for their coworkers. Leadership isn't the responsibility of just one or two people; it has to be there throughout the organization, top to bottom, not just with bosses and supervisors. You need to look for people who exemplify leadership in their daily lives. If you can foster that, you'll begin to tap a tremendous source of energy.

Finding Team Leaders

Not long ago I heard Bo Schembechler, the former University of Michigan football coach, give a fantastic speech about how he did his worst job of coaching with his most outstanding team. The team's captain was a great kid, but dissension had built up, and the team unexpectedly lost a game to South Carolina and then barely beat Northwestern. One of Bo's assistant coaches told him the players were grumbling about being worked too hard. Bo called the captain in, and the kid admitted that he was one of those complaining and said he thought a number of things were being handled the wrong way.

As Bo listened, he realized that he'd never once called the

captain aside and explained why the hard work was necessary and how important his role was — that the whole team
would take their lead from his view of the coaching staff, the
importance of discipline, and so on. As soon as that young
captain became a more positive force as a leader for the rest
of the team, Michigan had a fantastic year. Bo admitted that
his mistake in not talking to the captain earlier had cost the
team the national championship.

Most companies and businesses can be like that football
team. They have a great squad of people, with potential
leaders sprinkled throughout. No matter what size operation
you have, leaders are always present. With the right motiva-
tion, direction, and support, they can help your company
become world-class. Employee involvement, participative
management, and worker empowerment will help you find
leaders in unexpected places. Leadership should come from
whoever has the inclination to lead and is accepted by others
as a leader, not just the people who are anointed from above.
To help real leaders emerge, get the teams going. Give each
and every one of them a lot of power. Encourage experimentation, and keep the energy level stoked up.

What qualities will a team leader have? First of all, he's not
a complainer. He takes the initiative, makes positive suggestions, and helps others on a regular basis. He's got a lot of
energy and is truly interested in what's going on. Because he's
got confidence in himself, he's willing to say, "This idea may
sound nutty, but does anybody think we could go this route?"
A leader on a team isn't afraid to dare, to try ideas out loud,
and when others do the same, he has a knack for responding
clearly and rationally so the dialogue continues.

A leader instinctively knows how to criticize someone's
idea without insulting that person. In some cases, she might

even adopt a British approach and pose a critical suggestion in the form of an innocent question. For instance, if Marie has a bad idea for a new product, a leader might say, "Well, Marie suggested this route. What are the pros and cons of this idea?" As the cons are mentioned, Marie will see why her idea might not work. That's a good way of deflecting poor ideas without making someone feel bad.

Using Teams to Innovate

It's important for managers and executives of both large companies and small businesses to drop in on various operations and help people form teams. Shortly before I became Ford's president, we introduced the Lincoln Continental Mark VI. Basically, the Mark VI had lost its appeal as a stylish luxury car, and it was hard to tell any difference between the way it rode and the way the Lincoln Town Car rode. We obviously needed a new car fast. I asked the engineers to plan a session to brainstorm how to include as much improvement as possible in the ride and handling of the Mark. We met at a garage with hoists so we could look at cars with different suspensions and talk through our ideas. We examined every successful approach that anyone had ever dreamed of. That energized people into working as a group to figure out a solution, and eventually we came up with a way of installing an electronically controlled air suspension for the new Mark VII without totally redesigning the car. Going out to that garage and the subsequent follow-up work convinced me that we could plan to use this innovation, and we wound up adding a big improvement to the Mark VII. That experience, which came in the middle of a financially disastrous period, assured me that the talent inside Ford was grade A, especially when people pulled together. It also proved that a team of people, when given the power, can do outstanding work.

When teams are forming, it's easy to leave out some key people. For instance, you should look for ways to get your marketing staff to play a role in the idea side of the business. These people are usually not brought in until much later in the process, but sometimes researchers and product designers do not realize how appealing what they have might be to the customer. For that reason, it's good to have marketing people around to recognize the potential in things a research or engineering type might even discard.

One good example of this involved a computer developed in the 1960s at Xerox Corporation's Palo Alto Research Center. Dubbed the Alto, it was the world's first true personal computer, but the researchers had a tough time recognizing its potential. Accustomed to their high-powered IBM machines, they didn't think anyone would want a $3,000 desktop model. But a marketing person might have seen the possibilities immediately. That's why engineers and research scientists should show their ideas to a team of people from various departments, including marketing. Someone who is out selling your product or service, who's interacting directly with customers, is likely to spot opportunities that no one else will.

If your goal is to get as many people as you can to contribute to a project, team meetings are good for bringing out the best in even the quietest people. A facilitator can pull these people aside and say, "Explain to us once more what you're trying to do. What's good about this idea? Let's see what we need to sell it — and we'll come up with a proposal to make it fly." The finest team players do just this. It's the opposite of falling back on that age-old response "Show me your numbers. And if they prove x return on investment and y return on sales and fit into our budget constraints, we might do it." That's dead wrong.

Often you can sense that you're dealing with a potentially great idea, one that could yield tremendous profits or quality improvements. But going ahead with it and failing could break your budget or even your company. What do you do then? Instead of doing nothing, you can try piloting — testing the idea or innovation on a small scale before you commit a lot of money and resources to it. Every company should set aside funds for this. At Ford, we allotted funds for an experimental robotics center so that suppliers could bring in a robot and work with any Ford division to determine whether it could improve a production process. That proved to be a useful effort, and led to an assortment of new applications.

But keep in mind that startling improvements in your company or workplace won't come from a one-armed robot. They will emanate from your most precious resource: your people. If you encourage a more cooperative atmosphere, leaders will emerge throughout your organization. These team players will be the kind of folks who are always open to new ideas and can spot and nurture breakthrough products such as the Ford Mustang or the Xerox Alto.

People are the best source of innovation and ideas. If you figure out how to draw on that, your organization will develop the harmony of Dr. Deming's symphony orchestra.

8

The Manager's Role

All too often in business, as well as in our personal lives, people we genuinely like or admire have no idea how we feel about them, because we tend to keep it a secret. We think, "Why do I have to say anything positive? I haven't said anything critical." Sometimes when we say nice things to someone, there's also something critical in our remarks. When that happens, all the person hears is the neutral or negative part. What we forget is that human beings need positive reinforcement. We thrive on it — in a marriage, with friends, in education, and in business.

The more difficult the circumstances are, the greater the pressure and strain, the more important it is for a manager or coach to make positive comments to his or her employees or players. That certainly was the situation in the U.S. auto industry throughout the early 1980s. People badly needed to know that their hard work was noticed, that their technical abilities were admired. As managers, we had to tell them, "If you just keep going the way you're going, we'll make some real headway." And the tougher things get, the more you have to say that.

Here's a story that illustrates my point. In the midst of Ford's worst period in the 1980s, the Lincoln-Mercury division was having even more trouble than most. Sales were way down, and morale was terrible. We had to do something fast or risk seeing the collapse of a division that was a great potential source of profits. Red Poling asked a man named Gordon MacKenzie, who had climbed the ladder of sales positions and was then the head of the sales group for all the North American Ford vehicles, to go back to the division and turn the place around. In essence, he would voluntarily take a demotion to do this. But Red and I agreed that if anyone could bring Lincoln-Mercury back, it was Gordy. As far as salary, bonuses, and stock options were concerned, we treated Gordy as if he were still in the higher-level job, but we knew that he was likely to be at Lincoln-Mercury until he retired.

When Gordy moved over to Lincoln-Mercury, the place was in bad shape. An autocrat might have been extremely critical and relied on issuing orders. But Gordy was a team player whose approach was to say, "You guys are the best. You just amaze me. You are fantastic." He was such a cheerleader. Each step of the way, he brought the whole staff together. The environment quickly shifted from a negative to a positive one. Ben Lever, who had just returned from running Ford in Japan, was at Lincoln-Mercury when Gordy took charge and began to turn things around. To this day, Ben says it was one of the most exhilarating experiences he's ever had. If your company is trying to revitalize, what you need is a series of Gordy MacKenzies — a bunch of people who will go out there and get everybody excited about the challenges they face.

To encourage people, I used to write a lot of handwritten notes. I'd just scribble them on a memo pad or the corner of a letter and pass them along. There's something magical about sending memos in your own handwriting. Actually, the best thing a manager can do is pick up the phone and take a minute to thank someone or say, "I was really impressed with what you did." You just have to make a practice of saying "attaboy" or "attagirl" almost every day. You can't set aside an hour or so every Tuesday to write thank-you notes (at least I can't). You have to establish a pattern of taking, say, ten minutes every day to do something to boost the people who work for you. I would argue that these are the most important ten minutes of your day.

The best way to reward a lower-level employee involvement team is to praise its members publicly. Take them out to dinner and let the other people in the company know you're doing it. I also believe in rewarding people financially for their efforts, but managers tend to overemphasize the importance of money as a way of praising people. If you work at it, you can overcome the inhibitions you have about commenting on performance — and truly try to be helpful. This environment can be a big help when a manager needs to talk to coworkers about the need for improvement. If you've been routinely commenting in a favorable way, it opens the door for constructive suggestions. If you haven't been doing this, your constructive suggestions are apt to come out sounding like criticism.

Should a manager ever criticize his or her subordinates? For mistreating other people, acting illegally, lying, or having a blatant lack of interest in the company's well-being, I say most definitely. But a manager should never criticize someone for making a simple mistake, and no matter what, you should absolutely never criticize someone in public. I can't think of any excuse for that. Aside from how wrong it is to do that to another human being, the damage you do to the group is immeasurable. Everybody hears it and thinks, "Get back in the trenches. Don't speak up. Don't expose yourself to that." It's equally wrong to criticize someone behind his back; only rarely will he not hear about it, and the fact that you weren't honest and direct with him is even more damaging. I'm amazed how many people still try to manage that way.

The more senior your position is, the more careful you have to be about what you say. I was often asked why Ford didn't sell a sports car. My response was always "I'm cheering our guys on. I'd love to sell a sports car. I hope they can find a way." I was pretty sure the idea wouldn't come to anything, but as CEO I didn't want to send a negative signal to somebody who just might come up with a plan that could work. You never know where those ideas will materialize; you don't want to squelch anyone.

So why has Ford decided against making a true sports car so far? It starts with the fact that you have to have a goal of building a car that can stack up against the Porsches and Mercedes SLs. Thinking about anything other than a world-class sports car is simply unacceptable. Anybody who buys one is going to be shelling out an extraordinary amount of money to sit in a cramped space and get his hands on a lot of power and performance that most drivers never use. Even smash-hit, lower-priced two-seaters such as the Mazda Miata are limited in their appeal. Wealthy people might want one as a toy, and some young people will put up with them, but that's about it. When you consider all of that, it's hard to make money on a true sports car unless you sell it for around $100,000.

At this point, Mazda is selling a little more than 40,000 Miatas a year. Ford builds six million vehicles a year. When you recognize that you can't do everything and that you have to make choices, 40,000 vehicles with small profits may not be worth concentrating on. Mazda's leaders must believe that their success with the Miata will help their company's image and increase the sales of other Mazda models.

Falling on Anything but Deaf Ears

Too many managers never listen to others. They think their role is to come up with some creative ideas, write down some actions so that people can implement them, call a meeting, and say, "Here's what we're going to do, and here's who does each item." That'll get you only as far as your own mind can take you. Not only are you just one person, but if you're the boss, you can almost always be certain of one thing: when you walk into any meeting, you're probably going to be the person who knows the least. Maybe you will have read about the issue to be discussed, but there is bound to be more knowledge in the minds of the other people as a group than in yours. For that reason, it's a mistake to go in saying, "I have no problem with items five, six, eight, and ten on our agenda, but you'd better be ready for a fight on numbers three and four."

In the old days, people tended to come to meetings with their ducks in a row — all the people who supported their particular side of an issue all lined up. I remember that some other managers once chastised me after a meeting because I had dared to change my opinion after I heard what was presented. "Boy, we sure can't count on you," they said, proving that they had come in convinced that they knew who was voting for their side and what decision would be made in the end. That presumption was bad enough, but more disturbing was how closed they were to the possibility that they might discover a new idea in that meeting.

It's important for a manager to have as open a mind as possible — or at least to appear to — and to listen to what others have to say. If you have an opinion, one of the worst things you can do is let anyone know what it is. When people working under you know what you're thinking, they become inhibited about having different thoughts, and any chance of having a free-ranging discussion is pretty much killed. It's often best to poll the group: "Sonja, what do you think? Pat, good idea or bad idea?" The managers at Ford did that sort of thing all the time. It takes a lot of time, energy, and consistency to convince people that this exchange of ideas is helpful rather than a threat, but the difference in what comes out of a meeting will prove that it's worth doing.

The manager is ultimately the decision-maker in most cases, but in a team atmosphere, it's also his or her role to act as a listener and to solicit the group's ideas and plans. We had to shake people into that way of thinking and convince them that nothing was wrong with walking out of a meeting room with a totally different plan from the one they went in with. Managers who use their ears and listen will open a marvelous window to find out what's happening in the real world. One of the nicest notes I received when I retired was from Phil Benton, now Ford's president, who thanked me for creating a more open atmosphere, one that permitted free participation and discussion and fostered an ability to act independently.

Showing a desire to listen triggers some important actions. Several years ago, I confessed to knowing nothing about office computer systems. I said that I would have to trust our computer systems experts when it came to buying the equipment. I was so in the dark about what we were doing that I arranged a series of get-togethers on the subject. After that, a lot of people admitted that they didn't know what they were doing either. We made progress basically because I admitted I was ignorant and I wanted to learn.

Often the most important thing a manager can say is "I don't know." You'd be amazed how stimulating it is when a management type says, "I don't understand what you just said. I'm in way over my head." If the boss will admit that, he or she frees up other people to do the same. I can remember a number of occasions when some refreshing discussions started that way.

It's tough for a boss to tell his subordinates that they know more about something than he does and to run with their instincts on something. He has to have the self-confidence to trust and empower the people below him in the company hierarchy. Managers who lack this confidence are reluctant to give away power, because it means they're letting go of their ability to exercise control over other people as well as what they see as proof of their personal value.

People who are blindly ambitious tend to avoid sharing power as well. I've never thought it was necessary to be overly ambitious to get ahead in your career. I like to tell young people that the best way to work on a particular assignment is to set out to do it better than anyone has ever done it before. Concentrate all your energies on that, and the rest will take care of itself. Don't pay attention to some person down the hall who's ahead of you in the hierarchy; don't nuzzle up to some superior just for the sake of moving forward. I don't remember ever lobbying for a promotion. In fact, I was often angry when I was moved out of a job that I enjoyed.

Checking In with Reality

It's easy for managers, particularly at upper levels, to be far removed from what's actually happening in their companies. They tend to deal with only a few people, and those will primarily be their favorite staff members. This is a very autocratic approach and leaves management totally out of touch with people.

These managers love to hear themselves talk, and soon the people who work for them start thinking that what the boss yearns for is love and flattery. (If that's the case, believe me, he or she will get inundated with it.) People who work for autocrats also begin to shrug their shoulders whenever the boss talks, saying to themselves, "Well, we're in for another lecture now. . . . Is the meeting over? Did I miss anything?" In this kind of atmosphere, an idea will be acted on only if the boss thought of it. Because of this, any actions taken will usually be halfhearted.

Even managers who are team-oriented have a difficult time maintaining an objective sense of how things are going, what the weaknesses are, what should be happening differently. The higher up a manager gets, the more a sense of isolation inevitably sets in. For me, that was perhaps the most difficult fact to deal with when I became president and then CEO at Ford. People just stopped calling me; I had to call them. I've never figured out exactly why that happened; I suppose it stemmed from a respect for the position.

How does a manager stay in touch with reality? Get out of your office and visit people around your company or business. Talk to the workers on the front lines. Another great reality check is to test your product or service yourself. Engineers asked me my opinion about one car versus another all the time, and I had this nagging feeling that I wasn't consistent in how I test-drove a car or truck. On a handling course, I would catch myself going faster — say, five to eight miles per hour faster — in one car than another. By driving at two different speeds, I was losing the ability to sense the subtle but real differences between the cars. I wanted to be able to test-drive cars back to back and compare them accurately in a sophisticated fashion. I figured that if I were better at driving a car, I would also be better able to understand and interpret what people were telling me about various automobiles.

Mike Kranefus, our performance program manager, suggested that I spend some time with Bob Bondurant, who ran a professional driving school in California. It took a lot of effort to do this privately, but I wound up spending three days with Bob. It's amazing how much you can learn about driving correctly and why cars handle the way they do in just three days. Bob talked me through the fundamentals, chalkboard-style, of what happens when a driver accelerates, brakes, and steers; he also explained how the dynamics work when the driver goes through turns and how the biggest no-no is to apply the brakes while you're turning. Primarily, I found out what a mediocre a driver I was (and still am). But I did learn how to be consistent, which helped me tell the engineers what I liked and didn't like about a car with some confidence that my reaction was accurate. More important, my ability to check the cars knowledgeably sent a message that I was sincerely interested in what the engineers were working on and their efforts to improve the quality of our products.

Another reality check was visiting with dealers, who are our closest contact with the customers who buy our cars.

Early in my career, when I was in product planning, I put together an advisory team of dealers to help me plan the cars of the future. Throughout my career the dealers were a great help to me, especially Bob Tasca in Seekonk, Massachusetts. Bob is such a magnificent salesman that at last count he had been asked more than fifty times to take on other franchises. But he turned them all down, which shows what an intensely loyal dealer he is. He also has a terrific sense of what customers like.

Throughout the 1980s, Bob worked for Ford as a consultant more than he did for himself; his sons ran the business while he helped us. Many people at Ford thought that Bob and I were in constant contact and that he was my eyes and ears and even my spokesperson. Actually, we saw each other or talked on the phone no more than three or four times a year. But we had such similar perspectives about what should go into Ford cars that people noticed how the things both of us said sounded the same.

Bob's big campaign at the beginning of the decade was to improve our luxury cars. He started by going out to our Wixom, Michigan, Lincoln plant to talk to the people there. I'm sure some of them must have thought, "Who is this guy, anyway? Just because he's a swift seller doesn't mean he knows much about how to assemble cars." But Bob made himself a part of the Ford team, primarily by selling himself to people — one at a time. If he saw that his presence was bothering someone (usually an executive), he'd find a way to meet with that person and talk things through. He built up a network of supporters sprinkled throughout engineering, manufacturing, and marketing — people who recognized that Bob has a real knack for knowing what should be in an automobile.

Staying in touch with our dealers was a constant reminder that we weren't making products for ourselves; we were making them for our customers. After years of dealing first-hand with the people who buy and actually drive cars, and having a natural love for cars, Bob had an invaluable sense of what characteristics and features the customers want. He was also extremely good at pointing out the importance of fit and finish. Bob believes a car should look almost handcrafted, and that gaps around the doors should never vary in width and should be as small as possible.

Jackie Stewart, the international race-car champion, was also extremely helpful to me as a manager. Jackie has an almost instinctive sense for spotting what's right or wrong about an automobile — the way it handles, how it rides, the engine's responsiveness. He is also extremely good at ergo-nomics, which has to do with the positioning of the seats, controls, and gauges in relation to the driver. For obvious reasons, it's important for a driver not to have to take his or her eyes off the road to turn up the heat or adjust the windshield wipers. Jackie helped me refine my idea about building a "driver's car."

He also told me that he noticed Alain Prost, who recently surpassed him as the record-holder of Grand Prix champion-ships, driving an Acura Legend coupe. Prost owns all sorts of cars — Mercedes, BMWs, Porsches — but according to Jack-ie, he prefers the Legend because it makes him feel more competent as a driver than any other car. "Imagine that," Jackie said. "Here's the finest driver in the world, and he still prefers a car because it makes him feel even more competent as a driver." This really struck me.

One other individual who helped me a lot was Sotoo Tatsumi, who is now CEO of Japan's Sumitomo Bank. Mr.

Tatsumi came to Ford in 1977 with the idea of developing a close cooperation between Ford and the Toyo Kogyo Corporation, which later became known as Mazda. (Ford currently owns 25 percent of Mazda; Sumitomo Bank is Mazda's banker and, along with other Sumitomo companies, owns about 11 percent of Mazda's stock.)

As Ford's relationship with Mazda evolved, there was a lot of concern that the whole deal would be beneficial only to the Japanese — that they would get all of our technology and we'd end up with nothing but a supplier relationship with them. Just to be sure that this was not the case, we began doing an annual assessment on the partnership, and we determined that it was very fair. Generally speaking, Mazda learned from Ford in the product design area — such things as the control of emissions through electronic engine and other systems. And Ford has learned a lot from Mazda about improving our systems for better precision in manufacturing processes.

Over the years, Mr. Tatsumi was invaluable to me. He shared his views with me on what was happening inside his country and on Japan's relationships with other companies and nations. Mr. Tatsumi, who takes a long-term view of most things, often talked about what he saw unfolding in the automotive industry. Then he would ask me what I thought, with hard questions like "Do you think it would be smart for Ford to move down a different path?" After a while, I concluded that though he definitely had his own agenda, I didn't have to be wary of him. He is a man of great integrity, and he frequently helped us resolve disagreements with Mazda.

During my trips to Japan, Mr. Tatsumi helped me to behave in a way that made the Japanese people comfortable with me. He and I had a meal a couple of times a year with one of the leaders of Mazda. At Mr. Tatsumi's suggestion, most of the real issues that related to Ford and Mazda were settled at a lower level before our meetings. Americans tend to be confrontational in negotiations, but the Japanese hate all-out debate, because there's too much potential for losing face if someone is forced to give in. Mr. Tatsumi also helped me see how much the Japanese value private dinners and the friendliness that surrounds sharing a meal and drinks together. As is well known, the Japanese don't like to rush things. If there's business to discuss, it doesn't come out until pretty late in the evening, and then the participants go through the agenda informally. Mr. Tatsumi arranged a number of meetings for me with Japanese business leaders whom I might not have met otherwise. As anyone who has done any business in Japan knows, it's extremely important to build personal and lasting relationships with the people you're dealing with.

When we were putting together our plans for the Taurus, my friendship with Mr. Tatsumi helped Ford develop a relationship with Yamaha. We assumed that Yamaha couldn't work with us, because they already had an arrangement with Toyota and didn't have the capacity to produce more. Through his contacts with a lot of Japanese companies, Mr. Tatsumi knew that Yamaha had some engineering and production facilities available, and he suggested that we talk to them about building a special high-performance engine for the Taurus (which came to be the Taurus SHO). He took the necessary steps for us to be sure this arrangement would not be seen as a problem by the Japanese government or other Japanese companies. He also helped us develop a variety of beneficial cooperative relationships with Nissan, including cooperation in Australia and a jointly developed minivan that will soon be available in the United States.

Ford's relationship with the Sumitomo Bank on financial matters isn't important now, but it could be in the future. When the bank decided that it wanted a presence in the American investment banking business, Mr. Tatsumi picked Goldman, Sachs specifically because it has been Ford's major investment banking firm since 1956. Sumitomo bought a sizable stake in the firm, even though it's purely an investment at this point. All of this shows why I think my personal association with Mr. Tatsumi has been extremely valuable.

Learning from Your Critics: The Media

Reporters can be great sounding boards, and they will tell you exactly what they think more often than some of the people inside the company will. Two categories of media cover business: the general press, and special-interest magazines and trade journals. In the auto business, the special-interest magazines include what we call the "buff" publications, such as *Car & Driver, Motor Trend, Road & Track,* and *Automobile.*

Right after I became Ford's president, I put a lot of emphasis on getting in touch with the people at the buff magazines and trying to create a team atmosphere with them. Ford hadn't gotten a halfway favorable review from any of these publications in years. I found that one quick way to get an update on what was happening out in the car market, and what we weren't doing, was to ask some of these magazines' writers what they thought of our products. When it came to judging what customers would like, these people were some of the most knowledgeable around. They tend to like automobiles and trucks that go to the extreme in acceleration, braking, and other performance values, and they know the good stuff when they drive it. That's why I always tried to get their thoughts about a model as early in the process as possible.

I made the rounds and talked to as many journalists as I could. I also surprised some writers by meeting with them at their offices. Apparently, they'd never seen the president of any U.S. automotive company do that before. Reporters who covered Ford used to think that nobody above a certain level in engineering really cared what they thought about our cars. No one ever showed them prototypes or asked them questions.

When we were just getting started on the 1983 Thunderbird, a very important car for us, I tried out some of the design ideas on the writers. We assembled a picture book to show them, and as I leafed through it, I explained what we were trying to do. I think they appreciated getting a peek at something that was actually in the works at Ford, instead of just being shown sketches of cars we were dreaming about.

Once, when I was showing some journalists a prototype of a turbo coupe T-bird with a manual transmission, I asked them if they thought there would be a demand for this T-bird with an automatic transmission. Most Americans prefer automatic, but our marketing people were afraid that it wouldn't go over well, primarily because turbo-charging an engine doesn't make much sense if you are going to use an automatic transmission with it. You need to have the control over shifting gears that a manual transmission gives you to gain a significant performance benefit. But those of us who had driven the test model with an automatic transmission thought it was kind of fun. I asked the writers to take it out and see what they thought of it.

I have to admit I was a little afraid they were going to laugh at us — and at the car. Well, they didn't exactly give it a standing ovation, but just the fact that they didn't tell us we were out of our minds even to consider such a car played a big role in our decision to go ahead with it. Also, giving them this early look, a year and a half before we introduced the car, prevented it from being such a shocker to them when it came out. I was happy when they reviewed the automatic turbo T-bird and were kind to it. The car sold pretty well too, which again told me that these guys know what they're talking about.

Consumer Reports is very important to the automotive industry, and to just about everybody trying to sell anything. An amazing number of people read this magazine, and many of them keep back copies around so that anyone who's in the market for a car, for instance, can check how a particular make and brand compares to the competition. *Consumer Reports* does this with just about everything you can think of, from stereos to kitchen appliances to hotels. For a long time, Ford's attitude toward *Consumer Reports* was to hope that no one was paying any attention to it and it would just go away. Well, it didn't — not by a long shot. Now Ford regularly sends an engineer to the magazine, and the company always has someone available to answer a reviewer's questions. Our people are certainly not so naive as to think we can influence the opinions of the journalists at this magazine, who have a high standard of objectivity to maintain. But if they ever misunderstand something or need additional information, we want to be there to help clear things up.

Consumer Reports does provide its readers with very valuable information about various products, including cars. However, the one element it has never been able to quantify — and probably nobody can — is the emotional side of a customer's reaction to an automobile. The facts and figures stick to the logical, cold, analytical aspects of a car and miss the emotional appeal that makes people want a really sporty car, say, even when they know it has a poor maintenance record.

I also had a good bit of contact with the general press. They provided a different kind of reality check, mostly about issues such as safety and the environment. Their questions helped me understand the broad topics the public was focusing on and what was puzzling average customers. If I didn't have a well-thought-out viewpoint to answer these questions, I knew I needed to develop one.

The writers at West Coast publications were particularly helpful to me, because they were so completely removed from the automotive industry. They were probably the most objective sounding boards of all, because they truly had no stake in whether a car was made by a Japanese company or an American one. In addition, whatever they wrote was taken seriously — California is the nation's trendsetter for cars. Back in the late 1970s, these journalists recognized and wrote about how boring American-made cars were and how exciting and practical the ones from Japan were. In turn, they gave Ford the credit we deserved when we started turning around the quality and appeal of our automobiles in the mid-1980s. Our new cars sold like gangbusters in the West, despite the prominence that the Japanese had built up out there. At times, we even surpassed General Motors overall and became the number-one brand in the West, and that helped us throughout the country.

Editorial boards at general-interest publications can help you, too. A conversation over lunch with editors at *Forbes,* the *Wall Street Journal,* or one of the Detroit papers gave me a chance to explain what I was trying to accomplish at Ford. As we were getting employee involvement, participative management, and the teams under way inside the company, a lot of people on the outside were saying, "Something's going on over at Ford," but they didn't understand it. I thought it was important to explain what we were doing. Journalists often wanted to know about Ford's bleak financial picture, especially in the early '80s, but I made a point of talking about our efforts to improve the way our employees worked together. I'd start going on about how powerful the teamwork philosophy is; I'm sure these writers must have joked among themselves, "Are we up to another dose of Petersen's teamwork lecture?" In time the press became interested in our efforts, but it was only after many of us had repeated the important points and themes several times.

The press is important to any company or organization, because in so many cases it serves as the communication link between you and your customers. A lot of what reporters have to write about is negative; when bad things happen, it's news. And that's when unfriendly feelings can build up in your relationship with the media and spoil your ability to communicate. When it comes to that, the oil companies take the cake. In late 1990, when gas prices soared, the companies didn't explain why — at least, not to me. I assume that there was a reason and that they would like their customers to know what it was, but I never saw an item explaining it in the papers or magazines.

My approach to the media was to be as open as possible and to let employees speak out on a variety of subjects. Every company has to take positions on important issues — a hike in the gasoline tax, for instance, for us — and let its employees know where it stands. Sharing this information with your employees gives them a starting point when reporters ask questions about those issues. I believe if you give your people a good foundation concerning the company's position and the reason for it, you can trust them to express themselves well in whatever way comes most naturally to them. I never tried to control what anyone at Ford said in an interview, and I happen to think we came out quite well in the press.

Whenever I saw one of our people on TV or read someone's name in the papers, I took it as an opportunity to call him or her to say, "Caught you on TV. Great job," or "Saw your interview in *Automotive News*. Good work." As long as this is happening with people who know what they're talking about, encouraging them is also part of moving responsibility down in your organization.

When managers talk to the press about a success story, they should make every effort to give the team the credit. Imagine what happens when a whole group of people who worked together on something see their manager quoted in the paper about how proud he is of himself for pulling it off, attributing the achievements to his own know-how and talent. I'm sure most people can think of a circumstance in which they haven't gotten the recognition they deserved, and know how devastating it can be. Giving the team credit energizes them for the next big effort, and is one way to reinforce their sense that their work is worth something.

When Ford was going through a period of record earnings in the mid-1980s, we always let our vice president and treasurer act as our spokesperson for press releases on company finances. Not having the CEO or the chief operating officer handle those press conferences sent a message that the company recognized that these achievements didn't belong just to the top people. If finances are what the news is about, the financial member of the team should be the one who talks. That person is the expert and has all the information.

Lately, because the auto industry is in a slump, the financial people have had a lot of bad news to explain. When the news about any actions of the company is bad, the manager in charge has to take responsibility publicly. He's the one who chose to delegate authority to the people beneath him, and after all, it's his job to make sure the system functions correctly. So he takes the blame when something goes wrong. That's consistent with my belief that you never criticize people in public. You can't build a team, empower them with responsibility, then abandon them the moment something goes wrong, blaming them for mistakes you should have prevented them from making. Far too often I've seen people fall into the trap of wanting to be the spokesperson when the news is good and delegating that role when it's bad.

Helen Petrauskas, Ford's vice president for environmental and safety engineering, is absolutely terrific with the press, and she has an equally good rapport with government agencies. No matter what she is confronted with, she tackles it openly and with total integrity. Because she's cooperative and straightforward, she is trusted by the people she deals with. For me, that is the ultimate goal.

Teaming with the Union

In the past, Ford's relationship with the United Auto Workers union was extremely confrontational. Before 1980 the union leaders thought the only way to advance their cause was through an us-versus-them approach. Contract talks turned into adversarial contests. The union leaders were driven to get all they could out of management, rarely (if ever) worrying about the company's ongoing competitiveness. As time went by, hourly workers stopped looking to Ford for leadership and tried to find it in the union instead. In this kind of atmosphere, any management efforts to change things almost always died before they got off the ground.

That all began to change around 1980, primarily when Don Ephlin came over from General Motors to head the union at Ford. The American auto industry, and especially Ford, was fortunate to have Don playing the role that he did in the crucial years of the early 1980s. He was a real maverick among the union bosses, because he believed that the union and management could have a more productive relationship if they cooperated than if they worked against each other. At some point in his life, he decided that people should be given a voice in improving the quality of their work lives. It's difficult to know how someone develops a way of thinking that can break away from past traditions like that, but Don definitely did, and it played a large part in Ford's transformation.

Don's temperament is quite different from what you'd expect; you might think he'd be loud and pushy, but he's actually soft-spoken and moderate. In all my experiences with him, I can't recall a time when he ever preached to me. I always felt that he was a consultant and colleague, never an adversary. Don also had the full support of Doug Fraser, the UAW president, who gave him a good deal of latitude. It was also fortunate that we had just appointed a new man, Pete Pestillo, to negotiate with the UAW on behalf of management. Having two people who were relatively new to the situation created a fertile environment for change.

In the past, when the labor contract was up for renewal

every three years, all of us on the management side at Ford would practically hold our breath waiting to find out how much the labor relations staff had given away in the bargaining process. There was usually a lot of squabbling over various issues, and Ford was just as guilty of doing things the wrong way as the union was. But the negotiations in 1982 took a different turn. At one key point, Pete Pestillo suggested that I meet privately with Don Ephlin. This was quite an unusual thing to do, because before Don's arrival, almost all negotiations with the union leaders were handled strictly by the company's labor relations staff. Of course, that meant the union rarely talked with the people running the company, myself included.

Don and Pete had made some good progress, but I was worried that the contract wouldn't give us enough relief at a time when the company was losing a lot of money. Don and I talked for a long time, not really about specifics but as a way of setting a tone of cooperation and trust. I expressed how I felt, and Don responded by saying how confident he was that the programs tied to teamwork, employee involvement, and participative management would lead to levels of improvement greater than I could imagine and more lucrative than our financial people could put a number on. This was consistent with his faith that when you create a safe, congenial environment where people can work in harmony, you're going to get greater productivity, efficiency, and quality. He also pointed out that an atmosphere like that allows people to start talking to each other, and what they'll discuss is getting rid of problems, which, in addition to making their lives easier, cuts down on rework, defects, and all the hassles that problems cause. And that's one of the best ways to get higher quality and profits.

The 1982 Ford-UAW labor contract should go down in history as a real watershed. It said that Ford and the union agreed to work together to solve the serious problems we faced. The union agreed to forgo five cents of the hourly increase it wanted, provided the company would spend the money it saved on worker education and training that would be administered jointly by the company and the union. That included everything from teaching reading and writing to training workers in statistical process control.

The 1982 contract represented a remarkable change not only in the way contracts are negotiated but also in how they are written. They used to have a lot of legal language and contractese, but this one was in everyday English. Almost nothing about the language was punitive. It emphasized the importance of people and, implicitly, the idea that people were Ford's "second bottom line." To further that notion, I gave several talks after the contract was signed and ratified, saying, "Here at Ford, we're not just driven by the financial bottom line; there is now a second bottom line, which concerns how we treat people."

In the mid-1980s, Don Ephlin was moved to head up the General Motors union and Steve Yokich became the UAW's leader at Ford. Steve's appointment worried us, because in the past he had presided over some long strikes in the agricultural equipment industry, and he had quite a reputation as a hard-nosed leader. He was also clearly on the path to the presidency of the UAW, so we were concerned that his political ambition might prevent him from cooperating with us.

Steve had not been exposed to employee involvement and therefore was wary about its potential effect on the union organization. It was only a little while before he recognized how engrained EI was at Ford, and he soon started supporting the process and becoming more cooperative in his approach to various issues. It wasn't long before he was cosigning all letters about employee involvement to the union-represented employees at Ford. He seemed to gain the respect and admiration of the thousands of people in the union very quickly. And although Steve had been an unknown factor to those of us in Ford's upper management structure, we also rapidly gained respect for the strength of his leadership and his integrity. Steve was a straight shooter at the negotiating table and in the end, his years at Ford turned out to be very constructive. He was followed by Ernie Lofton, the present UAW leader at Ford, who came up through the ranks of union representatives in our plants. Everybody liked Ernie, and the managers were comfortable with his appointment because we pretty much knew what we could expect from him and we liked what we had seen.

To win the union's support for the changes we wanted to make in the work atmosphere, we also had to have good relationships with the union representatives at each of the company's plants and divisions. In many ways, it's more difficult to maintain a good rapport at that level of the union, because a lot of political struggles take place there, and the individuals contending for leadership want as much power as possible. I'm sure that every UAW plant chairman who agreed with what we were doing was challenged by someone who said he was getting too cozy with the company. In some respects, we learned how well our approach to EI and PM was going over through the results of the union elections at our plants around the country. Some candidates who supported cooperation with the company lost, but more won.

I'm sure there are still some old-school labor candidates telling the rank and file, "Elect me and I will ride that SOB bareback, digging my spurs into his side every step of the way." But it's good to see that era drawing to a close.

We learned a lot in the 1980s about dealing with the union. First of all, we made great strides in our ability to communicate with the union's leadership. Openness was the key. We had always kept the details of our accounting confidential, and though we didn't open the books completely, we did give the union leaders much more information than we had in the past, so they could clearly see what had to be accomplished. The union leaders have to be convinced that you're telling them the truth about your competitive situation if you want to have any hope that they will work with you. Otherwise, they'll just keep pounding on you, and neither of you will get anywhere.

Selling the Truth in Advertising

Throughout the 1980s, Ford's advertising tried to establish basic themes about the company, primarily that quality is indeed "job one." We also presented the idea of teamwork, using real Ford people in our ads. The current campaigns flash back to 1982: a supervisor says, "That's what I said then, and that's what I say now: at Ford, quality is job one." Our overall corporate advertising in the '80s heavily emphasized people, leaving the real product promotions to the individual divisions — Ford, Mercury, and so on. Since we were linking people throughout the company with teamwork and quality, that's what we emphasized in our advertising.

As Ford's president, I spent a lot of time working with our in-house advertising staff and with the creative people at the outside agencies who did the ad campaigns for us. I didn't really meddle in design and color — things the agency people knew more about than I did — but I objected to the hyperbole they often used and their attempts to portray Ford cars as being "very unique." They sometimes used doctored photographs, like Hollywood glamour photos, in which a special lens subtly stretched the car. I got together with the executive managers at the company's advertising agencies and told them, "You have to show our cars and trucks as they naturally are. There's no need to stretch them or to smear Vaseline on the lens to get that filmy look. Don't alter the color with some special lighting to make it a deeper red. Just show our red."

It took awhile for the tone of our ads to change, because so much hype had crept in. But when the advertising team saw that integrity was mainly what we wanted to stress, I think they came to enjoy working for us. One thing I probably overdid was my request to emphasize the dynamic element of our product — the fact that people don't buy a car just to park it in their driveway. I always wanted to show our cars in motion.

Lee Iacocca appears in a lot of Chrysler ads. He has become a good performer; he's really learned how to act and does a professional job. Lee's ads did a lot of good for Chrysler in the '80s, but I'm not sure if they are still effective now. Most of the time, using the head of the company in advertising is a bad move. You run the risk of not communicating as effectively as you need to just so you can keep feeding the ego of one individual. At one point, someone in advertising wanted to use one of the young descendants of Henry Ford in our ads. I voted against it, because I thought it went against our emphasis on the team. They knew better than to ask me to appear in ads. It's much more important to stress the team effort that goes into your products than one individual — particularly if he happens to run the company.

9

Working at the Top — and Helping Others Get There

Some people believe that the CEO's entire obligation is to serve shareholders. They think that all his or her other responsibilities should be subordinated to making profits and boosting the company's stock, usually with a short-range focus. I agree that the CEO has a strong obligation to shareholders, but I part company with a lot of CEOs over how that is best done. I seldom opened the paper and looked at Ford's stock price. And though I did explain what Ford was trying to do to the Wall Street analysts who recommend stocks to millions of shareholders, and although knowledgeable Ford people were certainly in touch with analysts frequently, there were only two occasions when I as the CEO talked one on one to a Wall Street analyst.

I also never spent a lot of time studying daily automotive sales. That kind of report is inaccurate; it tells you only how you're doing right then and is too short-term for a CEO to concentrate on. Even the quarterly earnings report has little to do with the thinking you have to do to devise a five- or ten-year plan. The CEO is the person responsible for keeping the company or business on a successful long-term track. This requires sound strategies for the future, a realistic business plan, and effective steps to implement them. I believe that if you work to improve the whole people side of the business and to develop your products and services so that you are delivering real value to customers, profits will come in the end.

Until Ford introduced the Taurus in 1986, any financial gains and quality improvements pretty much had to come without major help from new plants or technology. By revamping the systems we already had, particularly our relationships with employees, we made dramatic gains in productivity, efficiency, quality, and profitability. Still, we were criticized for not investing in the future. People said, "You're doing all these things with your employees, but you're not building any new manufacturing plants. Your financial results look better, but you'll be paying the piper in the end." At that time, General Motors was spending heavily on technology and building a number of new plants; it had just announced its plans for a major new manufacturing complex in Tennessee to build the Saturn, which was the first American franchise with a new name and new dealers and no consumer base since Ford introduced the Edsel. There was a lot of speculation that GM was going to roll right over Ford because of all this major spending.

I agree that investing in new plants and in equipment that incorporates the latest technologies and processes can be money well spent, but it is extremely important that you first get the people side of your enterprise working effectively by creating an environment that is open, free of fear, and conducive to individual initiative and change. Additionally, you should be sure that your processes are compatible with the equipment you are selecting, so you lessen the risk of applying all the latest engineering and scientific breakthroughs to systems that are needlessly complicated or flawed and that will plague you with problems. In short, don't automate until you've certified the soundness of your process.

It is also important to be sure that there is a good fit between the new equipment and your employees. Have you trained your people in the skills they need, regardless of what kind of equipment they'll be using? For example, do they know how to apply statistical process control? Will they feel comfortable working with the equipment? Is it user-friendly? Do your employees understand how it works, and are they convinced it will help them do a better job? Even with all this effort, you are still not home free, because real problems will inevitably arise as the new equipment leads you to newer ways of doing things. But when all your equipment and processes have been installed and are functioning, you and your people will know that you have taken the right steps for the long run, and that they will pay great dividends.

Toyota and Nissan followed different routes in the 1970s and early 1980s. Nissan invested a great deal of money in automating its plants and eliminating jobs; Toyota concentrated on training its people and encouraging teamwork. Our people came back from Japan and told us that these companies were like two different worlds at that time. If you wanted to see a plant where everything kept running after you turned out the lights and went home, Nissan was the place to go. But if you were looking for a plant that worked like a finely tuned watch, that was Toyota. There were still lots of people in the Toyota plants, using no more advanced equipment than was normally seen in the United States. I believe that Toyota was wise in its more conservative approach to automation, evidenced by the fact that Toyota is the most efficient auto company, it makes high-quality cars, and it is very profitable.

Judging the ability of employees to take on change is one of the toughest jobs a CEO faces. I found that it was best not to make that kind of decision by myself. Although I called on my own experience, I also used the knowledge of other managers who had worked their way up through the company. Even if the organization is fairly large, one or more of the top group will probably have worked in every major department, which means the CEO can utilize a rich mix of firsthand knowledge to help make such decisions. But generalists — the generic manager — with no technical skills or background in the core of the business, can't possibly have the expertise to make these judgments. On a number of occasions, Red Poling and I concluded that people were trying to do too much, and we asked them to take on less than what they were volunteering to do. The main reason we were able to make these decisions was that we had experience working in the core parts of the company.

Setting Priorities

When a new CEO or company president takes charge, he or she should probably start by sitting in on all the existing meetings to find out what's going on inside the organization. If the company is in such bad shape that it's barely functioning, the CEO obviously has to deal with that first, by delving deep into the firm's finances and the basics of the business. That's known as crisis management, and we did a lot of it at

Ford when I became president and chief operating officer in 1980. At a large company like Ford, the COO's job is mostly internal. He has to bore into the operations and work directly with managers and employees throughout the company, which is what I did for the first half of the 1980s, before I was named chairman and chief executive officer.

Part of the CEO's job is to support the COO, but the person in this position also has to pay attention to external forces such as mounting national budget and trade deficits, environmental issues, exchange rates, and any other big-picture issues that affect the company. (Unfortunately, outside forces are almost always negative.) The CEO has to establish a vision and direction for the company and do everything he can to get every employee to support them. It's important that he let his priorities be known and that his goals be clear and apparent. And he has to express himself positively. When Jimmy Carter shared his doubts with the nation, he lost his image as a leader.

Ford's statement of its mission, values, and guiding principles, which I discussed in Chapter 1, was a great way of establishing our company vision, particularly because it did so in a straightforward and public manner. An important step we took in making the statement the official guiding principle behind the "new Ford" occurred at a 1984 worldwide management meeting. Just before this meeting, the board had decided on the makeup of the next management team, which included my promotion to chairman, beginning in February 1985. The board had also just approved our statement on mission, values, and guiding principles. Henry Ford II had retired by then, but I asked him to come back and speak at the management meeting. The subject he chose was the company's new statement. This was certainly an act of support for me and for the continuation of the programs I had been behind as COO. After his talk, we passed on the stage, and he said, "Well, Pete, I hope I gave your mission statement a good send-off." Actually, it was a major declaration and had a great impact on thousands of our top people. Henry always tried to be extremely supportive. He was the strongest, most vocal supporter of my predecessor, former Ford chairman Phil Caldwell, during the toughest of times.

In addition to management meetings, a CEO's schedule tends to revolve around the cycle of board meetings. Ford has ten board meetings a year. (I remain a member of the boards at Dow Jones, which has eight meetings a year, and Hewlett-Packard and Boeing, which have six each.) There tends to be a natural work flow from meeting to meeting. I suggest that if possible, your company should schedule the board meeting and all the recurring committee meetings in one week, so that the top managers who must attend most of these meetings are free for close to three weeks a month to run their businesses and to get out of their offices and talk to people. Every upper-level manager has to function through other people, and that's hard to do if he is constantly interrupting his schedule, including travel, to come back for yet another committee meeting. And if he doesn't have a clear understanding of what his organization is doing, his contributions to the top meetings aren't worth as much. It's also extremely important for employees to see the managers and to know who they are.

It may seem that the CEO's job is far from the levels where teamwork and participative management take place, but the CEO can set an example by adhering to those ideas at every meeting he attends. First, that's the way he should conduct himself, and second, he should ask questions repeatedly about what progress is being made. When the top person is seen to do that, it increases the likelihood that others will do the same thing with their subordinates, which will help spread these new approaches throughout the company.

Building Leadership

One of the most important jobs a CEO or any other upper-level manager has is identifying people within the organization who have great potential and grooming them to become leaders of the company. At Ford, we arranged for the Policy and Strategy Committee — the CEO and the company's top officers — to meet regularly and talk about hundreds of executives in the company. There was a lot of serious discussion and debate in these meetings over the leadership question, and we made ourselves agree as a group about the best career paths for two or three hundred topnotch people. Each committee member then followed the same process in his or her particular area.

We also made an effort to identify the unusual individuals who showed the potential to attain the very highest levels of management. Once we identified such a person, he or she couldn't be given a new assignment without the specific agreement of the Policy and Strategy Committee. We wanted to be sure these people had a chance to gain a broad range of experience so they would have a legitimate opportunity to be among the leaders of Ford. This process pleased me, because instead of leaving the decisions up to individual managers in each of the functional areas, we made the executives actually running the company a part of the promotion and leadership discussion.

Beyond talking about the more senior executives, a CEO and upper-level managers should find ways to have contact with up-and-comers, to get to know them and to find out what they are interested in doing. Often years go by without anyone's saying a word to these people about how highly valued they are or how the company can help them advance their careers. I think executives should always be out there telling the bright and motivated younger people about the possibilities for their further growth. However, don't take this too far regarding specific promotions or particular jobs, because there's the danger of setting up your employees for disappointment if things don't work out.

Occasionally, very talented people aren't particularly interested in being promoted or taking on a manager's position. They prefer to stay in their own area of expertise, particularly in technical fields such as computer science and engineering. Companies often make the mistake of ignoring these people. I strongly recommend creating what many people call a "dual ladder" reward system, in which there are two parallel lines of advancement, one for managers and another for technically skilled people. Both groups should have the opportunity for advancement in salary as well as other benefits and rewards. This system tells the technically skilled people that they are as valuable as managers. And who knows, they could change their minds and wind up becoming leaders in the company.

If you're at a fairly large company, or even a medium-size one, you should make a dedicated effort to move your potential leaders around the organization. (And if you're a multinational, experience abroad can be invaluable.) All managers should gain experience in departments outside their own area of expertise: a finance person should spend some time in manufacturing, and a manufacturing person in finance. I also strongly believe that at some point in their lives, all managers should work on what I call the hard side of the business; if it's an industrial firm, they need to experience the actual process of developing and manufacturing the product, and if it's a service business, they should work in the part that has direct contact with customers. People who spend their entire careers on the soft side — for instance, at staff work in planning, finance, or external affairs — never really know what's going on in the heart of the company.

When you begin to look for ways to broaden people's experience, you might want to make sure you don't have rules in place that prevent managers from interviewing people who work in other departments. What a destructive blocker that is. Sometimes companies have a policy that prevents a manager from talking to someone in another department about a job unless a promotion is involved. In other words, you can't talk about a sideways move. That's also wrong. Often the best way to move people to give them more experience is laterally, and occasionally you will even need to move them somewhat downward.

To be useful, assignments outside a manager's area of expertise have to be meaningful, and they have to last more than a couple of months. A lot of companies fall into the trap of making token assignments, in effect saying, "It looks like this person is headed for the top, so we'd better dip him in manufacturing, and dip him in Europe, to give him that aura of having been seasoned everywhere." Red Poling says that you have to spend at least four years in a position to get anything out of it. Of course, he recognizes that if you try to stay four years in each of the posts inside a big company, you'll run out of years. But selected key assignments of long duration are a must.

Exposing potential leaders to a broad range of experiences within a company allows them to develop themselves. As Ed Deming likes to say, three things determine a person's ability to be a leader in any organization: his position or rank, his knowledge, and his personality. The first is hard for people to control, because it won't change until they get a promotion or a demotion. But they can certainly work on the other two areas, particularly if they are given the chance to enhance their knowledge of how the organization functions and what it must do to serve customers better. If a person has worked on the factory floor, she'll be better able to detect the pitfalls and opportunities in an idea proposed by someone who has never worked there. The higher a person goes in any organization, the more important it is for her to have a good base of knowledge. Without it, she will find herself lost in many conversations and often in reading documents and memos about issues on which she is supposed to make decisions.

In retrospect, I was fortunate to work for a huge multinational corporation where the opportunity for multiple careers exists right within the company. Not that many organizations offer that opportunity. But when I look back now, I think I changed jobs too often. I held more than fifteen positions in my first twenty years at Ford. If you change jobs too quickly, you waste a lot of time, because just when you've learned where the bathroom is and who's who in the pecking order, you move on to something new. It's a dilemma: your early years are also the time in your career when it is easiest to get a variety of experience. In my case, I was often the designated start-up person, the one who began new functions. I learned a lot, but frequently I wasn't around long enough to see how it all turned out. Still, the experience I gained in so many positions gave me unusual insight into the company.

Last, you might want to look for ways to encourage your more reserved higher-level managers to break out of their shells and become leaders. We didn't do that enough at Ford, though I do remember asking Tom Page, the head of the diversified products operation, who played such a key role in getting participative management off the ground, to take a Dale Carnegie course early in his career. Tom is extremely bright, but he's soft-spoken. He has so many talents that I felt it was important to urge him to do something to feel more comfortable in groups and in making presentations. Dale Carnegie teaches people those skills and helps them become more outgoing when dealing with others. I'm not sure how much the course helped, but Tom eventually became a member of the board and a real leader in the transformation at Ford. Another way of helping people gain confidence is by convincing them to take public speaking assignments and to talk with journalists on behalf of the company.

Hiring Team Players

Executives and managers rarely get together and ask themselves how good they have been at hiring people over the past five years. Did they get the right people, and if so, where did those people come from? Instead of having a plan of action for hiring, I think, most companies hire people on an ad hoc basis. As a result, people randomly enter the company in various departments, and nobody measures the overall adequacy of the process; very often, no one keeps track of what happens to people after they are hired.

I see several problems with the way hiring is normally handled. First of all, in most organizations the personnel department tends to perform this function. Personnel people can try their best, but they are removed from what's going on from day to day in a given work area. They might not have a complete understanding of what the job is and which skills are needed. Often the people working in the department know nothing more than the names of the people who are hired. Imagine walking into a company on your first day and having to introduce yourself to your boss and your new coworkers.

Another problem is that the people doing the hiring lean in the direction of "safe hires," selecting applicants who fit into a mold, who have the "book" definition of the right background for the job. I can understand going that route in most cases, but unless you keep yourself open to the possibility of hiring someone who doesn't exactly fit what you're looking for, you're likely to miss a lot of opportunities to bring creative innovators into your business.

At Ford, the top officers discussed specific colleges and universities that we wanted to target for hiring new people. We then assigned an executive sponsor to each school and asked him or her to take a team of people there to interview potential recruits. The team looks for people who have done well academically, but they also look for traits and experiences that indicate that someone will be a good team player. Of course, it would be impossible to come up with a foolproof checklist for determining whether or not a person is a team player, but you can get a pretty good idea if you make a conscious effort to do so. Did he participate in activities at the school or in the community? Is his attitude positive? Is he confident? Was he a member of any club, or did he play team sports? Does he have a curiosity about things?

Hiring is certainly not an exact science. But if a company believes that its people are its greatest resource, the top executives must make responsibility for hiring a priority. It's important that someone who understands the job and believes in the overall company philosophy of teamwork be involved in recruiting and hiring the people who constitute the organization's future.

Shooting for the Top

If you decide you want to be a CEO or run a relatively large operation someday, first you have to determine what you really want to do based on your genuine interests. I don't see how someone can be truly successful doing something that doesn't appeal to him.

It's also important to let your superiors know early on that your goal is to get as much experience as you can. Of course you want promotions, although you don't want to develop a reputation for being impatient. There's nothing wrong, however, with asking for a different job that will give you broader experience. It can be a real drawback if you move up too many rungs of the ladder in one part of the company without getting experience anywhere else. If you move up too many levels in your primary area of interest, you might wind up having to take a demotion so you can gain experience in another area. Definitely try to get a job, or several, on the hard side of the business. Work on designing or making the product or in the service area, and sell yourself to your superiors with results.

People who lack confidence in their abilities often make the mistake of thinking that they'll move ahead faster if they criticize others who are in line for the same position they want. Or they ally themselves with someone they think is heading for the top. Both of these tactics might give you successful results in the short term, but whenever I've seen people go that route, sooner or later the bottom falls out on them.

I also recommend to middle managers that they get in the habit of forming their own opinions about difficult and big-picture issues. It's not a bad idea to ask yourself, "What would I do if I were running this company? What should our strategy be? What would I urge this company, or this industry, or this country, to do about extremely complex issues such as energy conservation and competitiveness?" It's good to develop the habit of thinking independently about major questions, even if your goal isn't necessarily to reach one of the top spots in the company. The process will lead you to a better understanding of what the company as a whole is faced with, what management is attempting to do, and what role you can play.

10

Redefining Quality

Everywhere you go lately, people are talking about quality as if it were something that had just been invented. In a way it has been — at least as we speak about it today. For a long time, Americans have known how to produce large quantities of goods; in many ways, that was how we won World War II. But recently some other countries have been outdoing us with quality. Fortunately, a number of U.S. companies have figured this out and are getting on the quality bandwagon. The quality revolution at companies like Ford has been long in coming, and a little walk through history is needed to understand it completely. Even though I am using cars as an example here, the same applies to any good or service.

In the 1950s and early 1960s, U.S. automakers enjoyed a seller's market. Cars and trucks didn't change much technically, and the way they were made was mighty simple. You opened the hood and it was all there. The spark plugs were lined up and easy to get at. You could take things apart yourself, check connections and clean them. The standard 1964 Mustang convertible, for instance, had a manual top, single-speed windshield wipers, a three-speed manual transmission, and a six-cylinder engine. It didn't even have outside rearview mirrors. (Don't think I have all those details memorized; I still own one of those cars.)

Back then you had to drive your new car slowly for a while to break it in, and you took the car in to your dealer regularly. If small things went wrong, they were fixed easily, and it seemed routine. And as long as the automaker had satisfied customers and the cars improved a little year by year, everything was fine.

Then things began to get complicated. In my career, the automatic transmission was born. We added air conditioning and power applications for windows, seats, steering, and brakes. Things began to fall apart when regulations came into play in the late 1960s. The government came at us from all sides: the Safety Act was passed in the mid-1960s, the new Clean Air Act was passed in 1970, and standards for automotive fuel economy were set. The auto industry no longer had control over its own destiny. The carmakers were busy incorporating a rapid flow of new technologies into cars and trucks, and there was a quantum jump in the complexity of the vehicles — all based on timing established by the regulators in Washington. I remember that when I was working on antilock brakes for extra-heavy trucks, we learned that the electronics involved could be affected by stray electronic signals from other sources, so we had to figure out what was in the airwaves in order to design the brakes.

But what brought quality absolutely to the forefront was the use of electronics to control all the functions of the engine. The engine, which had always been based on relatively simple electrical and mechanical actions, now was controlled by electronic signals created by fingernail-size computer chips, and that meant a car might grind to a halt because the electronics weren't right. And that problem was compounded by the fact that we were racing to keep up with government regulations and hadn't found the time to teach repairmen how to solve some extremely sophisticated computer-related problems in our cars. They didn't know how to troubleshoot an electronically controlled engine. Computer chips — also known as semiconductors — are extremely sophisticated devices. For instance, a state-of-the-art chip called a microprocessor can process up to five million instructions in a second. The cars weren't working dependably, and relatively few people knew how to fix them for certain. More and more owners had to come back several times for the same problem, and, predictably, they started to get mad.

From that point on, we had to improve the quality and reliability of our designs dramatically, and to do this we had to make our manufacturing processes far more dependable and consistent. Most of the early government regulations affected cars more than trucks, so our car engineers and product planners became totally consumed with meeting all the new laws. Not surprisingly, people's minds became regulation-driven instead of customer-driven. They began thinking that if the people of this country had a government that said, "This is the kind of car we want, regardless of what its performance is" — if they wanted a car that wouldn't get out of its own way, that stumbled when you tried to drive it, and that was clunky-looking, with 5 mph bumpers that jutted way out from the car — then that's what they were going to get. Of course, people's minds didn't totally shut down, and there were discussions and debates about new ideas. But we definitely weren't thinking enough about our customers.

For instance, let's say that everybody on a given design team was talking about meeting a new safety requirement involving the instrument panel and the steering wheel. Their job was to hold the design of the overall interior to a certain price tag, but the cost of the interior was $10 over that budget, and the work was already running maybe six weeks late. There was no time for basic redesign, because the final design prints had to be released. So the team would forget about adding extra features and eliminate some that were already in the design. Sometimes they would do away with carpeting in base models, or eliminate the armrests or the door pocket. The door pocket was expendable, right?

Anyway, that was the setting. It's hard to fault the people who went through it. All too often, they felt that they just didn't have the time to do things right. We didn't realize that disaster was going to strike the U.S. auto industry.

An Attack from All Sides

Essentially, foreign car manufacturers attacked the United States in three waves. Wave One came from Europe, primarily in the form of the Volkswagen Beetle in the '50s. That forced U.S. firms to reintroduce small cars. But the Beetle tried to be a Beetle forever. Volkswagen thought that keeping the same design was part of their mystique, but that was their mistake. The Beetle died rapidly when American small cars were introduced and the deutschemark strengthened.

Wave Two was an effort by the Japanese and the Europeans to bring in cars throughout the 1960s. The Japanese cars were unattractive and not very enjoyable to use; the Europeans chiefly exported sportier, up-market cars. Ford reacted by bringing out the Mustang. It had this rightness to it, a real sportiness, and it was fun to drive.

As the 1970s began, the quality of cars built in Europe, Japan, and the United States was essentially equal, in terms of defects and reliability. During the '70s, the quality of American and European cars seesawed: we'd have a nice improvement one year, then we'd slip. So the European and U.S. products were similar in quality when the decade ended, and the Americans thought that was quite an achievement in the face of all our government regulations. But the Japanese were creeping up on us by making steady, year-by-year, continuous improvement. It was a subtle thing at first, but over ten years — by the late 1970s — there was quite a gap. At first Japan's advantages in quality didn't seem to affect sales of American cars much. Ford's market share was just under 24 percent, and GM was still getting essentially half the market. The Japanese were worrisome, but their share was small. In the late winter and early spring of 1979, there was even a substantial backlog of little Japanese cars sitting at the ports. The Japanese were offering big incentives because the cars weren't selling; Americans wanted larger cars.

Then Wave Three hit, after the revolution in Iran in 1979 caused another energy crisis in this country (because of what was believed to be a shortage of gasoline). In my opinion, the permanent shift toward Japanese cars happened then, and actions taken by the U.S. government to deal with the energy crisis just exacerbated the problem. The government allocated gasoline state by state, but its strategy was based on old population numbers. As a result, the recent growth in some states, such as California, did not show up in the figures, and those states were starved for fuel. As the TV news showed motorists lining up at gas stations, the whole country came to believe we had a fuel shortage. There was no shortage in Topeka or in Rochester, New York, but people sure felt that there was. And that had a devastating effect on U.S. automakers. Customers almost immediately began switching to small, fuel-efficient cars made by the Japanese. Then they discovered that these cars were not only fuel-efficient, but nothing went wrong with them. They were inexpensive, reliable, and easy to maintain.

That wasn't our only problem during this period, however. America's younger and better-educated professionals — yuppies, they're often called — began buying BMWs, Mercedes, Volvos, and other European models in large numbers, simply because they liked the way they looked and performed. They recognized that these cars had a harder ride and required more effort to steer and brake than American cars did, but they liked the overall driving characteristics built into the design. Also, the price was right, because the value of the U.S. dollar compared to European currencies was soaring through the roof.

American carmakers began the 1980s being bashed by both sides. The Japanese sold fuel-efficient cars with few defects, taking a lead on the defect-free side of quality; the European models just felt right, and their makers capitalized on the excellence-in-design side of quality. Almost concurrently, the appeal of Ford products relative to other cars was very low. Everything was boxy, even the Mercury Cougar and the Thunderbird.

Ford had simply lost touch with the customer.

Getting It Right

For too many decades, Ford, as well as thousands of other U.S. companies, had a superficial and single-dimensional definition of quality that almost entirely concerned objective measurements, or the number of things that went wrong. Our biggest mistake was not being driven by what customers wanted and not making a disciplined effort to examine the subjective side — the intangible look and feel that attracts customers to particular cars. This became glaringly evident when we had to stop producing the Ford Fairmont in early 1983; it was probably the highest-quality car in our entire line in terms of defects, but it wasn't selling well, because customers just didn't like it.

In contrast to the situation in cars, the people in the truck operation, working in teams and listening to what customers were saying, kept their focus squarely on the customer. The truckers kept improving, reacting, getting information from both employees and customers. Their market research and styling research was better. Typical of that era was a man named John Frechtling, who was smart as the dickens but was considered too eccentric to work on cars. He just ate statistics up. He had stacks of paper everywhere, yet somehow knew where everything was. People like John, the irascible and curmudgeonly type, were characteristic of the employees who were moved out of cars and sent to work on trucks. But John was a wonderful resource, and he would not let people tinker with his information in a way that would alter its integrity. I remember vividly how much better the flow of information was; the truckers knew much more about what customers wanted. And Ford's truck market share remained strong.

The most important thing we learned this past decade is that all those elements that appeal to a customer, that are intangibly right, must be considered a part of the overall quality of the product. Look at a man's suit: what makes up the quality of that suit? Well, the fabric — it's good-looking and has a nice, soft feel. And the seams are sewn right. But then you have to look further. Is it slow to wrinkle? And do wrinkles hang out? That's just as important, if not more so. But you wouldn't discover that until you wore the suit awhile — that is, until you used it as a customer. We just hadn't made that connection as well as we should have.

In the mid-1980s, Mr. Yamamoto of Mazda described to me the concept the Japanese call *kansei,* which is the oneness of the product and the user. *Kansei* takes into account all the intangible things that make a customer feel both confident and right at home when he or she steps into a well-designed car. I told Mr. Yamamoto that we didn't have a name for it, but that was exactly what I had in mind when I described the "driver's car," and what Lew Veraldi and his team put into the design features of the Taurus.

At Ford, I became a nut when it came to quietness — especially the sound made by a car's engine. Ten years ago, when I was out walking, I could tell whether a car had been made in Japan, Europe, or the United States before I could see it, just by listening to the engine noise. A Honda or a Toyota made amazingly little noise cruising by. That, in the customer's mind, is a sign of quality. U.S. cars are a lot better now, but even today, I'm usually right when I guess where a car was made just by listening to it. Another sign of real quality for me is the care with which everything is laid out beneath the hood. I'm convinced that a beautiful engine compartment is a high-quality engine compartment, and I know many customers agree with me. I believe that numerous companies fall into the trap of taking less care with the less visible parts of their products, but the quality must be superior there as well.

Quality also means striving to provide your customers with products and services that go beyond their needs and truly surprise and delight them. That's where market research can be a misused resource. Average customers don't know what is possible if they haven't seen or heard of it. So if you merely deliver what they want at the moment, somebody else will put you out of business by offering more. Federal Express, for example, has succeeded because of a breakthrough — guaranteed overnight delivery — which apparently no one else thought was possible. And I'll bet that the people at Federal Express are worried that somebody somewhere is developing a way to deliver information even faster and more efficiently. If I were at Federal Express, I'd be wondering, "What's the next advance in this area?" I'd ask customers, "Is there something you wish you could do but you can't? Is there any possible way we could serve you better?" (I notice that United Parcel Service is selling the idea that they provide better Saturday delivery.)

Of course, market research that is done right can offer you a good understanding of your customers, but you can't take it too literally. The greatest errors in market research happen when you ask superficial questions that don't really probe what the customers think. You get nice quantitative research, but well-targeted, qualitative research, including face-to-face interaction with customers, can help you a lot more. I remember a story one engineer told me. He couldn't understand why customers didn't like one of our transmissions. He was certain that the component was properly designed and manufactured. But then he went out driving with several customers, who showed him how the transmission seemed to stumble or hitch a little. Once he understood their objection, he knew what to do to eliminate the problem. The engineer learned that quality is determined by what customers think about your product in actual use. That's why it's so smart to send people like engineers out to talk to customers on a routine basis.

Since I retired, I've been traveling a lot on commercial airlines instead of on corporate jets. I'm going to be a much better board member for Boeing now that I regularly use that company's products. I was recently talking to the people in Boeing's commercial airline division. They said a lot about the customer, but they were speaking about the 150 airlines that buy their planes, not about the passengers who use them. I asked them about the things I see as a passenger: seats that barely tilt back, if at all, and a lack of sufficient leg room; the utter chaos that goes on as passengers scramble for storage space for luggage in the inadequate overhead bins and hang-up racks; marginal galleys and restrooms. As we talked, they told me that by and large Boeing doesn't design the airplanes' interior; the airlines do that. They want control over the design, either so they can limit costs or so they can add features they think will increase their competitive advantage over other airlines. (I was recently in a 747-400 that has an electric control for tilting the seat back and bringing the leg rest into position. That airplane was to be delivered to — you guessed it — Japan Air Lines.) I suggested that passengers don't draw fine distinctions; if they don't like the final experience, they are just as likely to blame the manufacturer as the airline. Boeing's people might want to keep their hand in to make sure Boeing interiors are consistently liked and appreciated by the travelers who use them.

Another change we at Ford made in our thinking about quality was even tougher. We had to adopt the philosophy that quality is just as important internally as it is externally. In other words, everything you do inside a company, whether it's typing a letter, running an engineering analysis, or attaching a bolt, affects other employees, who are really your internal customers. The people who receive your work depend on you. If your work is bad, they can't do an excellent job either. If your work is incomplete, the next worker in the process has to complete it before he or she can go on to the following step. When this happens a lot, a tremendous amount of time is spent reworking things, and that is such a waste. So within any organization you have to keep two customers in mind: the internal customer, or everyone who will be affected by your work, and the external customer, the person who buys the final product or service. This kind of thinking can't be limited to people in manufacturing and customer service. It has to extend everywhere within your organization. I don't believe that it's possible to give your customers consistently excellent products if you allow shoddiness to exist anywhere. Striving for the highest quality must become a routine and natural way of life for your employees, no matter how close to or removed from the buying customer they are.

We also had to accept the fact that the old measures of quality, such as producing 99 percent defect-free parts, simply aren't good enough. Here in the United States, Bob Galvin, the former CEO of Motorola and now the chairman of that company's executive committee, really pioneered the idea of building products that are virtually perfect. The goal of Motorola's methodology, known as Six Sigma, is to ensure that products are free of defects a startling 99.99997 percent of the time. In some ways, the electronics industry can set such a dramatic goal because its products are based on computer chips, which are increasing impressively in processing power as well as improving steadily in quality. The vast majority of the chips, incidentally, are made by the Japanese.

Shooting for Six Sigma or perfection is helpful, because it's almost totally impossible to reach with your existing systems and processes. In other words, it makes you think about entirely new ways of doing things. Achieving this goal will be extremely difficult in the auto industry, however, because cars have dozens of highly complex systems: an electromechanical system that moves the car, a ride and handling system, safety systems, an emissions control system, a climate-control system, an entertainment system, and so on. A car is vastly more complicated than most products, and the sources of its parts and components are widely varied. For example, more than half the parts in a Ford car come from outside suppliers, which makes setting specific goals for quality improvement very difficult.

Even so, Ford took steps in that direction. In 1983 we created a prestigious award for suppliers, called the Q1 Award, which stands for "quality first." The award is very difficult to win. We rated suppliers with a complicated measurement system. A company had to score more than 70 (on a scale of 100) to qualify as a Ford supplier. To be a Q1 supplier, it had to have a score over 85 and use statistical process control — the quality improvement methodology taught by Ed Deming. At the beginning of 1990, the company raised the Q1 rating from 85 to 90 and required all new suppliers to have a Q1 rating. Starting in the 1992 model year, all suppliers — as well as all Ford operations — must have the Q1 rating or they will no longer do any business with Ford.

If your company is serious about quality improvement, you must ultimately strive for perfection. John Young of Hewlett-Packard drove his company to make products whose quality is ten times better today than it was ten years ago. Setting a specific target can be justified as a useful way to motivate a large body of people. If it's high enough, it will show them just how much they need to do and that they have to discover and implement entirely new ways of doing things. Some of your people will think that the job will be completed when the company reaches its target, but you have to emphasize that the work is never done; the organization needs to keep getting better year after year.

A big danger is not setting your goal high enough. Maybe you need to achieve a twentyfold improvement instead of a tenfold one. At Ford, we tended to underestimate how quickly the Japanese were improving, and many American companies make the same mistake. The questions you have to ask yourself are "Where does the competition stand today? With continuous improvement, where will it be ten or fifteen years from now?" Over and over again, you have to re-examine who in your field is really the best and whether you are chasing the right rabbit.

The secret to catching and surpassing the best is continuous improvement. In the 1980s, Ford managed to pass a good number of Japanese companies in the area of quality, but we still haven't exceeded the best. Right now, I rate Toyota the best, followed by Honda; and Mazda does a great job. The reason Ford caught up with the Japanese the way we did was not that we had some magical breakthrough in design or technology. The secret was steadiness of purpose: empowering people and buying into the idea of continuous improvement. The secret is making steady progress in everything you do.

In Long Beach, California, there are marks on a wall in a little house on Cedar Street. Those marks — probably beneath a dozen coats of paint — chronicle my growth inch by inch. Even though I wasn't able to control how fast my height increased, those marks were a real chart of my progress. I remember fondly the day I discovered I'd grown taller than the doorknob. I never would have gotten there if I had not been continuously getting taller.

Making Quality "Job One"

A lot of people like to use "total quality management," or TQM, as a catchphrase for a companywide effort to improve quality. Boeing calls its effort "continuous quality improvement"; at Ford it's called "total quality excellence." But TQM seems to be everybody's favorite these days. Some people moan that the terms are just fancy words for another program — another flavor of the month — that has no lasting value. That is certainly true if a company or an organization does a superficial job with the idea, by just hiring some consultant, holding a few meetings, and declaring itself a TQM company. Unfortunately, total quality management is a weapon that few companies really know how to use.

To back up what you say about quality improvement, you have to be obsessed with it night and day. Management has to commit itself to a never-ending search for ways of making sure that defects and errors never happen. A common mistake is to blame the work force. When workers aren't doing their jobs properly, most often it's because they have been given a faulty design or the wrong equipment or were not trained properly. Under those circumstances, they can't do a good job, no matter how hard they try.

Oftentimes when there's a small problem, such as a bad screw on a car door or an editing mistake in a newspaper, people put their attention entirely on the error instead of examining the process that allowed it to happen. Endlessly correcting little problems is not only frustrating, it doesn't lead to lasting improvement. You have to ask if you could make any change in the process to eliminate the chance for an error entirely. It's also wise to find ways to identify problems in "real time" — to pinpoint them precisely and immediately after they occur. At Ford, we encouraged plants to let workers, or selected individuals, shut down the assembly line when they spotted a problem. That helps keep a product problem from getting into a customer's hands, and if a change in the process is required, it is made immediately, not days or weeks later.

Design also plays a large role in the quality of the final product. Some say that as much as 80 percent of the quality of a given product is determined by its design. For years at Ford, the men who put the bumpers on the cars used something called a shim — a small piece of metal that looks a bit like a washer — to adjust the bumpers to make them look like they fit the car's body. We thought this quick-fix process was a perfectly fine way of overcoming variations from one car to the next.

Then along came the Japanese with the idea that if you designed the car right, all the parts would fit together right, which would save the costs of extra labor and added parts. The first car we jointly manufactured with the Japanese was the Laser, which was made in Australia. When the design information came in, there were no shims specified for adjusting bumpers. The Japanese design people expressed the view that if the design allowed so much variation that shimming was required to align the bumpers, we would almost certainly end up with erratic results. We would also never know if our manufacturing processes were improving, because the factory workers would be injecting more variability in the results by trying to make adjustments.

In this case, if people designed the parts with no provision for adjustments and the equipment and tools were set up to build the parts as specified, the bumpers would fit the car as the designers intended. If all that were true, assembling the products would be almost a no-brainer. A robot could do all the heavy work, and the shimmer could do a different job, one that actually produced something instead of correcting mistakes. Often people think that quality is determined on the factory floor, but in most cases it's determined up front, in product design. And management is responsible for making this happen.

Quality improvement frequently gets tough for people when costs enter the equation. All too often, good ideas that could improve quality are crushed by those who are terrified to spend a buck. Someone might have a suggestion that's worth trying, but it gets rejected because of the costs involved. For instance, if you have a $1 billion program to develop an $8,000 car, you might begin running into questions about whether to use a better exhaust system design that costs substantially more money. Management must not just dismiss that design simply because it is more expensive. Instead, the managers should permit the right team to study it to identify all of its benefits. What is it worth to the customer? The system might make it easier to build the car more efficiently, because it's easier to work with. It's possible that the design would be much more durable and would eliminate the need for parts normally used to reduce engine noise. That sort of probing can show you all sorts of reasons why what seems to be a relatively costly improvement will actually reduce overall costs and achieve dividends in quality as well.

The financial systems at most companies are simply unable to do sophisticated cost analyses. Typically, the benefits of superior quality, such as the value of improved customer loyalty, aren't factored in. A system is often simplified and improved in many ways that don't get added into the equation. Instead of making an attempt to figure these things in, people take the easy route of not trying new ideas because of cost considerations. If quality is your goal, the financial people in your company have to adjust their thinking about long-term, cost-versus-value measurements, so that value to your internal and external customers in relation to costs — not cutting costs — becomes the driving force behind every consideration they make.

Quality, then, is not determined simply by what it costs you to add a unique new feature, such as the cargo nets that hold groceries in the back of the Ford Taurus. Quality is what surprises and delights the customer.

Pockets of Progress

11

Going Global

Remember the days when people thought that the reason the Japanese were so successful was that their workers bounced out of bed, threw on their company uniforms, and ran out to do calisthenics together? It looked as if that wonderful Japanese culture spawned a natural camaraderie and a single-minded drive to win that no other country could possibly match. There was a time when I too bought some of that line of thinking, because it sounded plausible.

But after I examined what Japanese managers really do to get their workers to perform as they do, it seemed much less mysterious. And when I saw similar concepts put into practice here in America, I became convinced that Japan's miracle didn't have anything specifically to do with its culture. In fact, any manager who says that the ideas behind teamwork and participative management can work in another country but not in his or her own back yard is copping out. The secret to Japan's success can't be found in exercises or company songs. The calisthenics were dreamed up by Japanese managers as a way to reduce the risk of muscle pulls and strains, which are the most common injuries in factory work. The miracle is rooted in the basic philosophies outlined in this book, and they'll work as well in Barcelona and Düsseldorf as they do in Detroit and Tokyo.

Ford's experiences in Europe show that real progress can be made there, even if it happens differently in all of the various countries. Ford has sales companies in each of the Western European countries and manufacturing and assembly operations in many of them, the largest ones being in England, Germany, and Spain. For the past twenty-five years, all these operations have functioned as a single European organization, a fact that has forced people from a wide variety of cultures and nationalities to share ideas and look for ways to cooperate.

The Europeans have been quite successful at using participative management to improve relationships, even between people who speak different languages and who are from countries that have long-standing animosities toward each other. Since the mid-1980s, about seven hundred managers from Ford of Europe have attended a PM seminar similar to the one developed in the States by Nancy Badore. In fact, Nancy went over to Europe and taught several of them herself. This training has helped Ford's European managers work together and share the wonderful resources of the Germans, French, English, and Italians.

Some of the European managers are forming multinational teams to develop new products. For example, Ford's European Escort, which was introduced last fall, was the result of a five-year program led by designers and engineers based in England and Germany. Like Team Taurus, the Escort team eventually expanded to include almost 1,200 people before the car was completed. The small teams that develop products draw people from all of the Western European countries, and there's even a sprinkling of Americans here and there. As I mentioned earlier, program management — the team approach to developing new products — was actually started in our European operation. One of the great advantages of having a team with such diverse talents, both technically and culturally, is that it has the expertise and background to know how customer tastes will vary from France to Belgium, or from Eastern Europe to western Germany.

At this point, Ford of Europe appears to be much further along in product development through teams than any other operation outside the United States. It's clear from their behavior in the Senior Executive Program and the participative management seminar that Ford's European executives have been working hard in this area. When the American seminar leaders break everyone into discussion groups, the European managers often turn out to be such good facilitators that the instructors try to put one in each group. Because they have been running PM seminars for several years, the Europeans have had a lot of practice with these activities and are comfortable with them, and almost all the Europeans, no matter where they come from or what line of the business they're in, have good team-building skills. I've found that to be true of Germans, Belgians, Italians, Spaniards, Scandinavians, and the French and the British.

It might seem odd that these European managers are willing to support ideas imported from America, but there are several reasons why they do. They tend to think of American businesspeople as neutral parties who are uninvolved in intra-European disputes. Americans tend to forget how much rivalry exists between the French and the Germans and between the Italians and the British. It's not likely that these bitter feelings will fade away anytime soon. In a sense, Americans have the advantage in being viewed as outsiders who can step in and propose new ideas without being immediately second-guessed or criticized. In fact, Europeans have often told me that they like having Americans around when they discuss things in groups, because the Americans are sometimes able to prevent them from getting at loggerheads with one another.

Slower Progress in Employee Involvement

Even though so many different facets of participative management have been advanced in Europe, Ford's European managers have had more difficulty in establishing an employee involvement program, particularly in Britain. (Their success with PM underscores a point I made earlier: that employee involvement doesn't necessarily have to be up and running before you move on to other actions. You're trying to get people to cooperate and share ideas, which can begin at the management level anywhere in the company.) Ford has made repeated attempts to launch EI in its European facilities, especially in Britain and Germany, and so far has had only mixed results.

Over the years, the labor-management relationship in Britain has been extremely difficult, primarily because every manufacturing plant has a large number of unions, which are forever squaring off with one another for power. Also, British laws put very few teeth in the labor contracts, which seem to allow workers to go on strike or to cause disruptions without any reason to believe they'll face any sort of punishment.

In the early 1980s, some of Ford's consultants tried to convince the British labor chiefs to launch an employee involvement program based on what we were doing in America. However, nothing ever got off the ground, because the union leaders were so opposed to the idea. They wouldn't even come to the United States to talk with the United Auto Workers and see firsthand what was going on. There was finally a glimmer of light a couple of years ago, when the UAW convinced some of the British union chiefs to come over for a visit, and I'm hoping that EI will eventually take hold at the hourly level in our British plants.

Ford's British management team had some success with employee involvement among the salaried employees, particularly engineers, production foremen, and clerical staff managers, who are represented by different unions from the hourly employees. In 1985, after a lot of discussion, our British managers reached a formal agreement with the three relevant unions to give EI a shot among their membership. Steering committees were set up, teams were formed, and we made pretty good progress for the next few years at most of Ford's twenty-two British facilities. But after about three years, interest in the program began to slide, mostly because we were not able to expand employee involvement to the hourly workers. Around the end of the decade, the three unions representing the salaried employees withdrew from the contract that supported EI, arguing that it had gone about as far as it could. But even though the program no longer exists in a formal sense, the teams still meet on their own in about seven or eight of Ford's British plants, and the idea of employee involvement is still alive and well among salaried workers.

In Germany, Ford has made considerably more progress. Many people think of the Germans as autocratic, and that stereotype has had some basis in fact for much of their history, but for more than forty years they have been learning how to live with a closer relationship between management and labor. Germany has a government regulation known as codetermination, established after World War II, which requires every German firm to have an employee representative on the company's board. Not only has this helped foster the spirit of participative management, it has served to promote the idea of employee involvement.

All German workers up to the middle-management level are represented by a works council, which is similar to an American union (though it has a lot more clout). The head of the works council at each company has a seat on the company's board and votes on any matter that comes to the board. He or she also has the option of vetoing any worker training programs the council opposes. Therefore, it's almost pointless to push a program such as employee involvement before you have the work council's enthusiastic support. If you do get the council behind you, the chances are high that your effort will succeed.

To gain the council's trust and cooperation, leaders in Ford's employee involvement program invited council members to visit America in the mid-1980s to see what EI was all about. When the Germans came, they spent about ten days touring Ford assembly plants and talking with union leaders as well as management about the program's history. They were apparently so impressed with EI that they agreed to endorse it fully, and we were permitted to launch the program in Germany. Now every Ford facility in Germany has an EI steering committee and an EI coordinator. So far these groups have done a fair amount of cooperative work to improve the quality of Ford's products.

Heading Overseas

If your company is fortunate enough to have a European arm, the best way to get your employees there to support what you're trying to do is to share your vision with them and encourage them to support it. The last thing you should do is issue orders that they have to try all of this. If you can keep pounding away at it, eventually they will get started.

I remember visiting some of our European plants to talk about these ideas. Usually I did this after one of our quarterly meetings in Europe, but sometimes I made a special trip just to tour facilities and talk to people. Of course, talking with employees in a plant in Germany, Spain, France, or Belgium was difficult because of the language differences, but since Ford is an American company, I could usually find a few people who spoke English. Just as in the States, I could get a feel for what was happening by looking at people's faces and talking with them about whether their managers believed in the new philosophy. Generally, the teams I ran into there weren't very far along, and I could tell that some of the supervisors touring the plants with me still hadn't fully accepted the team concept. But I kept encouraging the teams and the managers, and I'm pleased to hear that real progress is being made.

It's fine for Americans to tell Europeans about what has worked here, and, frankly, the Europeans seem fairly receptive to it. They recognize that we've all been hit by many of the same problems and have been trying to hold our own against the Japanese. Having this in common helps American managers get people in the various countries to begin to work together and to set similar goals. But once people beyond our home base have been convinced to get started with improvement programs, you have to leave it up to them to decide what to do and how to do it. As we discovered at Ford, the British do something entirely different from what the Germans do, and I'm sure that people in other countries will take other paths.

Why Europe Is Important

I have said for some time that the world is now living in the Asian era. America's most critical industries — automobiles, computers, electronics, and even entertainment — will face their stiffest competition from Asia, particularly from Japan. But Americans who ignore Europe could be in for a rude awakening. At the end of 1992, the twelve countries in the European Community — Germany, Italy, France, the Netherlands, Spain, Belgium, Denmark, the United Kingdom, Luxembourg, Portugal, Greece, and Ireland — will start an accelerated program to eliminate most of the trade barriers among themselves. In an economic sense, that process, widely known as "Europe 1992," could lead to a "United States of Europe," in which business people can increasingly operate under a set of rules and regulations that will govern the entire community. For example, truckers will be able to cross the border between Germany and Denmark, or take the underwater tunnel from Britain to France, without having to stop at a checkpoint. Once the 1992 process is completed, companies will be able to sell identical cars, TVs, computers, telephones, and all other products in all countries in the community. A service firm based in any of those countries will be able to operate in any other without obtaining special licenses. There is even a strong push to replace the various currencies with a single European currency, possibly the "ecu," which is already used in some business transactions.

So far the 1992 program has led to hundreds of mergers and acquisitions, because companies want to become pan-European powerhouses with the size and scope to battle American, Japanese, and other foreign rivals. That certainly is cause for concern for American multinational giants such as Ford, General Motors, and IBM, which have large European-based operations that have accounted for up to a third of their corporate profits in recent years. Ford has more than 60,000 employees in Germany alone, and has huge manufacturing and assembly operations at Halewood and Dagenham in the United Kingdom and at Valencia in Spain.

Medium-size and even small firms that are interested in exporting to Europe are going to find it tougher to compete. Some people fear that the European Community will set up quotas or tariffs to reduce imports and foster the growth of small European firms. I have no doubt there will be dramatic changes in the top five firms in many industrial, commercial, and financial business segments in Europe over the next few years. And the winners and survivors will be those who begin to prepare now.

American managers should not look at the 1992 program solely as a threat. It also will offer unprecedented opportunities for growth. After 1992, the EC will form a single market of 320 million people — 70 million more than the United States — with a gross national product considerably higher than ours. For the foreseeable future, the European Community will probably grow significantly faster than the U.S. economy, creating the largest common market in the history of the world. This will also be greatly fueled by the rebirth of Eastern Europe. Currently, millions of redevelopment dollars, as well as marks and yen, are flooding into reunified Germany, Hungary, Poland, and Czechoslovakia. American firms can participate in this rebuilding and should watch for places where they can tap markets in Eastern Europe, which are virtually virgin territory at this point.

As all of Europe attempts to lurch forward, there will be a growing need for all companies there — American-owned as well as European-based — to improve the efficiency of their factories, the quality of their products, and the productivity of their work forces. That's where employee involvement, participative management, and teamwork can be helpful.

Unilever is one European giant that is headed in that direction. With dual headquarters in Rotterdam and London, Unilever makes such brand names as Vaseline, Karl Lagerfeld, Elizabeth Arden, and Shedd's. I'm familiar with the company because I serve as an advisory director on Unilever's board of directors. In 1990 I participated in a meeting of the worldwide management team of the company's personal-care products group, which has been taking aggressive steps to adopt total quality management. As I listened to the team members talk about their quality program, I saw that they were doing many of the same things we did at Ford. Most of the managers I talked to have been through a participative management seminar, and I know they are beginning to nurture cooperation at the plant level as well. They've also visited American companies to see what we're up to with TQM. All the insights they've gained have been gathered into an excellent series of written reports that are shared with managers throughout the companies in the group.

As European companies pick up steam, these ideas will undoubtedly catch on, company by company and country by country. They may not even be referred to as EI, PM, and TQM, and I'm sure they will have a distinctive European flair. But it doesn't matter what terms you use or what language you speak, as long as management and workers of all varieties and personalities are communicating effectively and working together in a spirit of cooperation and teamwork.

12

Teamwork at Your Service

Every manufacturing company has a large number of people who work solely on the service side of the business. These are the employees who sell the product, process the bills, keep the financial records straight, and work in the customer service center. Of course, there are also tens of thousands of firms that do nothing but provide services, including banks, airlines, hotels, insurance agencies, and retail stores. Until recently, many people running these operations pretty much went about their business without paying much attention to the new ideas that were reshaping the factory floor. They had probably heard how statistical methods and teamwork programs were changing the way manufacturing companies operate, but they hadn't tried to apply these ideas themselves. If they haven't, I think they have missed the boat, because these ideas are just as applicable in the service sector as in manufacturing.

If introduced properly and used extensively, employee involvement and participative management will help any company improve the efficiency of its services and will make its employees better able to serve customers promptly. We all hate waiting in line at the bank or the grocery store or being put on hold while we are trying to correct a billing error or make an airline reservation. We also know how great it feels when a service operation is run properly, with few errors, and when we're treated with trust and respect by a waiter, a flight attendant, or a clerk in a department store. When service is good, it's usually an indication that the manager has created a positive atmosphere and has put in place processes that allow workers to make decisions and offer suggestions without worrying what the boss might think.

To improve a service operation, you should begin by following the same path that we did in manufacturing. Get some teams together in a few offices or stores and let employees start to talk about their problems. Don't worry about whether the discussions are sophisticated or whether the initial ideas people come up with are plausible. People who spend a lot of their lives sitting at a desk or standing behind a counter will learn from the experience, and will begin to understand that it's okay for everyone from a clerk to an office receptionist to suggest things that would make her work life easier, improve the company's productivity, and make customers happy.

At Ford, employee involvement is making progress in most of the service operations that support the manufacturing side of the business, as well as in the gigantic financial services group, a 26,000-employee division that has more than $120 billion in assets. This group is another great proving ground for these ideas, because much of it is almost totally independent from the car and truck business, and it is involved in a wide variety of businesses, from credit cards and insurance to car and home equity loans to leasing.

To keep tabs on how things developed on the service side, I

stayed in close touch with Ken Whipple, president of the financial services group. Ken has been an enthusiastic supporter of the cultural change at Ford, and he wholeheartedly endorses the notion that you can use these concepts to improve any service operation dramatically at a manufacturing giant like Ford or anywhere else.

At first, the hourly people in the financial services group focused on little annoyances and registered a string of complaints about everything from punching time clocks to having to park their cars a long way from their offices. Ken and his managers made it a habit to listen and not to criticize the teams' early suggestions. Some of the first office teams didn't work out well at all; the secretaries, for instance, didn't seem to come up with much, because they worked in different offices and didn't share many of the same problems or day-to-day tasks. With help from facilitators trained by the human resources department, the employees formed more logical teams, and gradually they began to focus on more meaningful suggestions that would make the group more productive, particularly when it came to cutting down on the mountains of paperwork.

Someone who was an expert on filing showed the others the best way to organize all their drawers and cabinets. A team in the credit department discussed the fact that managers were continually examining employees' "delinquency ratios" — the number of unpaid car loans each of them was responsible for. This led to a lot of wasted time, because some managers routinely sent their employees out to repossess the cars so they could take their delinquent customers off the record books and avoid being called on the carpet. Repossessing a car and reselling it is extremely expensive — it costs an automaker an average of $4,000 per car — and it should be avoided whenever possible. When that team realized that this was happening, a new practice was adopted in which managers looked at the delinquencies for the entire department, not for each employee. That discouraged people from repossessing cars simply to avoid the boss's wrath.

Beyond the EI teams, we taught participative management techniques and began encouraging people from different departments or financial chimneys — accounting, customer service, treasury — to get together and discuss ideas. The results were pretty impressive in several cases. For example, the people in the treasury department began talking with some people outside their department about the company's banking practices and how Ford borrowed money. At the time, the treasury managers typically went to the company's favorite commercial banker, figuring that all the big banks on Wall Street offered roughly the same interest rate. But as a result of talking to the outsiders, they became convinced that they should put the business up for bids and see whether any banks would offer a lower rate. Not only did we get a better rate then, but Ford has been asking banks to put in bids for loaning money to the company ever since.

We also brought together groups of people who worked in the same line of business but who had never cooperated before. Managers in the treasury office in Detroit, for instance, began meeting with the people who were out in the field loaning money to customers. They talked about how to save the company money as well as serve customers by shortening or extending the length of the company's loans. A treasury manager might be able to tell the field reps that the interest rates were currently a lot more attractive to the company if the loan covered a period of four years instead of five and that they should encourage customers to take out four-year loans. In turn, the people on the front lines could provide the treasury managers with up-to-date details on which loans customers preferred or could best afford. Because of those discussions, these two groups now work like a team.

A similar kind of idea-sharing and team-building will certainly help any service operation improve. You should strive to reach the point where employees in a given office or store automatically help one another and naturally bounce ideas off one another. If you haven't been doing that, your employees will continue to be irritated by superficial problems, which will hurt morale and lead to even greater inefficiency.

Statistics in Services

Many people running service businesses probably think that the work they do varies too much from day to day to benefit from statistical process control. But if you look closely, you're likely to discover that many of your business activities utilize the same repetitive processes almost every day. Federal Express sends more than 1.9 million packages around the country each day and guarantees overnight delivery; the airlines try to maintain a schedule of thousands of flights. These businesses have to find ways to ensure that the operation runs as perfectly as possible, just as a manufacturing business has to eliminate defects in the products it makes.

It's impossible to make a lasting improvement in quality in a service operation until you know what's going wrong in the system or processes you use. You know the questions you'd like to be able to answer and the problems you'd like to correct. The real question is, how do you do it? If you apply statistical thinking to the job, using statistics to study how it is being done, you can often pinpoint where the errors are occurring. Then you'll be in much better shape to find out why and correct your processes.

At Ford, the goal is to examine difficulties in every service activity, from accounting errors to the percentage of customers who were kept waiting longer than two minutes for a customer service representative. The effort to track down the source of the problem and change the process to reduce the chance of an error never ends. In customer service, we rearranged schedules to make sure that more employees were available at the right times, so that customers wouldn't be kept waiting on the phone too long. (A prompt response to a customer's problem can actually make him or her more loyal than a customer who has no problem at all.) We also grouped all the customer service reps in one location, so they could work on common problems and the managers could spend all of their time improving the systems these representatives use to help customers.

The most important step is to establish a strict set of standards for all your services and make sure that the number of errors doesn't go beyond that. But don't assume that once you've reached your absolute minimums, the job is finished. Your goal should be continuous improvement.

Obviously, it's difficult to measure quality performance in a setting where almost everything the workers and managers do relates to serving customers. One way in which Ford has tried to stay up on how it's doing is by routinely surveying customers and talking to them in focus groups. For instance, we set a standard that 90 percent of the people who borrow money from Ford Credit must be satisfied with the service they receive, and we check with those customers regularly to find out how they feel. The company also conducts interviews with car and truck buyers about our dealerships, and every dealer gets a report card on his or her performance. This rating plays an important part in determining which dealers receive the company's top quality award.

Customers used to tell us that they were badly treated by their dealers, but the dealers would blame us for not putting out a better automobile. We showed Jim Burke, then the chairman of the National Ford Dealer Council, and Eddie Soukup, who held the same position with the Lincoln-Mercury dealers, videotapes on which customers said how angry they were with the dealers and explained what they thought was so wrong. Jim didn't think his dealership had these problems, so we asked if we could talk to his customers. He was brave enough to let us. When we showed him the videotape of his customers criticizing the way they had been treated by his salesmen and his service shop, Jim realized that he had to change things. He and Eddie volunteered to lead a nationwide effort to improve customer relationships with dealers. That's when we started to make some progress, and there has been continuous improvement in this area ever since.

Technology to the Rescue

When you begin looking for ways to improve a given service process, remember that technology can be an enormous advantage. If you can do things faster and with fewer errors, you can be much more competitive. The U.S. Postal Service is rapidly automating by installing robots that can read the Zip Code on a letter or package; some hotels are speeding up the checkout process by letting guests fill out a form on an electronic monitor in the lobby or on the television screen in their room.

Ford's service managers are using teams to come up with similar improvements. Every year the Ford credit group provides customers with more than one million car loans. The people there developed a process that enables loan officers to approve a car loan on the spot if the customer meets a set of income, job status, and credit history criteria. The teams are trying to figure out how to do the same thing with applications for home mortgages. Normally a prospective home buyer waits a month or more for a mortgage to be approved, but the credit group wants to get that down to fifteen minutes or less.

The service managers who work with Ford dealers are using a time-saving bar code scanning system to keep track of the inventory of the company's cars. Now when someone from Ford goes out to the dealership to confirm that the cars and trucks arrived and to find out whether they are still on the dealer's lot or have been sold, he no longer has to write down the long serial numbers of each car. He simply runs a hand-held scanner across a plate to complete the inventory check.

Making People Smile

You cannot really force people to smile and be friendly to customers. If you try, they'll either fake it or it'll happen only when you're watching them. The best way to get your employees to present a cordial and happy appearance to your customers is to give them more responsibility, show them that they're trusted, and encourage them with praise and even financial rewards. This will help them to feel confident in themselves and be more likely to take on a more positive attitude, which customers will definitely notice.

When I walk into a restaurant or a store and see that everybody has a sour attitude, I blame the manager. The vast majority of the time, the grim look on people's faces tells me that the boss has not fostered a team atmosphere and hasn't done anything to guarantee that the employees aren't overworked or underappreciated. When a business is well managed, the people who work there tend to be pleasant and ready to serve. Frequently, they are also willing to pitch in on someone else's job if they need to instead of worrying only about themselves.

Customer service managers at Ford studied the way in which Federal Express empowers its workers to go to almost any extreme to please a valued customer. A lot of folks have undoubtedly heard the story about the local Federal Express manager who chartered a helicopter to deliver a package to a snowed-in mountain home. Obviously, you can't let people do that sort of thing all the time or you'll run out of money. However, that is the right idea. Management should establish a philosophy by which employees know that there are times when they should do whatever is needed to make a customer happy, even if it costs a buck or two.

At Ford's financial services group, management has been letting people use their own judgment more. The loan officers now have increased flexibility in working with delinquent customers on ways to avoid foreclosures. Managers are also free to encourage the people who work for them to operate this way. In one case, a local Ford credit manager gave his loan officers a $100 bill for each home equity loan made after-hours, as a reward for working overtime. (Ideally, of course, you should try to use a financial reward like that to recognize the work of an entire team, not just an individual.)

I would discourage companies from using some of the usual techniques of checking up on how well their employees are performing in customer service. A few companies hire "mystery shoppers" to make sure salesclerks are doing what management has ordered them to do. One department store even gives its mystery shoppers a "friendliness rating form" on which they grade employees on "smiling, greeting customers promptly, being helpful, using customers' names, and saying thank you." Some of these shoppers grade the salesclerks on levels of friendliness and later show the results to managers as well as the employees. Clerks who receive more than three "unfriendly" scores are sometimes fired.

This kind of evaluation system is dangerous, because it suggests a lack of trust on management's part and it almost forces workers to look over their shoulders in constant fear that the next person they talk to is a mystery shopper. Nobody can work well in a factory or a service business where distrust and fear prevail. Good managers don't need devices like this. They should be sure to let their employees know what they expect at the outset, and they should be able to tell who is doing a good job and who isn't. If customers are treated unfairly or unpleasantly, the manager will hear from them.

Another customer service practice that doesn't help much is the kind of simplistic rating forms you see in hotels, restaurants, and some retail stores — the ones that typically ask customers if all the employees did their jobs, if service was prompt and courteous, and what they'd like to see changed. Although it's true that companies might get an idea from those forms now and then, very few people will take the time to fill them out, and when they do, the information is usually quite superficial. Customers' complaints tend to be either pet peeves or the result of a one-time event you can't do anything about.

It seems to me that it's better to bring a small number of customers into focus groups on a routine basis and talk with them about their likes and dislikes, their problems or complaints, and what your competitors are doing that serves them better. That will give you a broader picture than just a yes-or-no checklist that grades how your service workers or your entire firm happened to perform on a particular day.

Pulling It All Together: The Associates

Ford owns an excellent service business called the Associates. This financial service giant, with $18 billion in assets and 8,000 employees, concentrates on home equity loans and truck financing and is the tenth or eleventh largest credit card provider in the United States. The folks at the Associates use a team approach from top to bottom. The top ten executives have a free and open relationship; without even thinking about it, they work like a team. They know all the details of their business and are among the most astute managers at Ford. Their operations have been growing so quickly that Ford can barely build facilities fast enough to house them. Life at the Associates is cooperative, and all the employees seem to know about their coworkers' sons and daughters and the other personal things people share in a team-based environment. It's part of their culture.

The Associates got to where it is because its management continually strives to empower people and is forever looking for ways to improve the operation. The managers there never make an important decision without hearing what their experts have to say. They also extensively use statistical process control, some of which they learned by studying the outstanding service operations at Motorola, Inc. The Associates provides the loans for people who buy Motorola's small consumer products, such as pagers and cellular phones.

Beyond serving customers quickly and efficiently, the Associates is much faster on its feet than other companies its size. That's important in a service firm, where the time it takes to get something into the market is dramatically shorter than it is in a manufacturing firm. A carmaker can spot a new concept and spend at least three years in research and development before getting a car based on it ready. In contrast, a service firm can put something new into the market in a matter of months or even weeks.

Lately, many companies have started offering their own credit cards. In an environment as hotly competitive as this, it's important for your people constantly to come up with ideas to make your services slightly better than those that everyone else is offering, and for them to serve customers in a friendly and more satisfying way. That's where the energetic and can-do attitude of the Associates offers a tremendous competitive advantage. I'm sure the company can get a credit card on the market in a matter of weeks when it wants to.

Any service firm that is trying to improve should do a little benchmarking, as manufacturing companies are starting to do. It should look at outstanding organizations such as the Associates and Federal Express to find out what works. In addition, it should do everything it can to promote the same cooperative environment and positive attitude that Ford is trying to nurture in its offices and plants.

13

Applying the Ideas Elsewhere

Shortly after I retired, I got a call from Admiral Frank Kelso, who had just been appointed the chief of naval operations for the United States. He was interested in applying the ideas we had used at Ford, including the concept of total quality management, to the navy. The admiral told me he wanted to change the way navy personnel work together, to get them to take more initiative in generating ideas instead of just taking orders from commanding officers. Admiral Kelso's call was similar to a lot of letters and calls I've received in recent years. People are deeply interested in what we achieved at Ford and wonder how they might be able to apply those ideas in their organizations. It's encouraging to know that people all over the nation want to use them, everywhere from the factory floor to retail shops to ships at sea.

After Admiral Kelso called, we got together for the better part of a day. He asked me if I thought he needed to create a master plan that would launch a quality improvement program, and if so, what that plan would involve and how he would get it started. Having grown up in the navy, he probably took it for granted that you have to issue a set of orders before anything can be accomplished. That's the military way. I told him that at Ford we hadn't really known anything about total quality management when we first got started. I explained how the NBC documentary "If Japan Can, Why Can't We?" had led me to meet with Dr. Deming, and I told him about our serious interest in employee involvement and how we had gotten inspired to make quality our number-one priority. I told him about the Richmond, California, parts depot where the hourly workers convinced their bosses to stay home for a week so they could prove they could run the place.

I suggested that Admiral Kelso might start the way we did at Ford and give some of his people at a small navy facility the freedom to experiment with these ideas by forming teams and beginning to tackle problems. We discussed the idea that a repair facility might be a logical starting point. "I bet you won't have much trouble finding a place where people are frustrated by all the rules they have to live by and have opinions about how to run it more effectively," I said. "Why don't you give it a try?" The admiral seemed to like the idea of starting out small and agreed to go that route.

In March 1991 we talked again, and he assured me that he was following through with his effort. The secretary of the navy had endorsed what the admiral now called his total quality leadership program. Kelso and his aides are experimenting at several small naval facilities scattered throughout the United States, and they are trying to adopt the philosophy that everyone in the navy, on shore or at sea, has a "customer" that he or she must be concerned about.

The navy is also trying use the team approach to come up with ways to deploy ships faster and more efficiently. In the old days, the captain alone bore the burden of going to sea on time. Now everyone from members of the maintenance crews to critical parts suppliers is a part of the deployment team. Kelso also told me that his counterpart in the air force has launched a similar quality program. The fact that these two men are beginning to use teamwork and the other ideas I'm advocating is a marvelous sign that the military is working toward becoming more efficient and quality-oriented.

At first it's hard to imagine how employee involvement might work in the military, because enlisted personnel are so used to following orders that they might hesitate before suggesting an idea or questioning an officer's opinion. Admiral Kelso and I agreed that orders must be obeyed, in much the same way that Ford managers, not the employees, have to make the final decisions in the company. But that doesn't mean that everyone in the navy has to sit around waiting to be told what to do. Even in the routine of military life, there's plenty of room for group discussion and suggestions before an officer decides what needs to be done and how to do it.

Obviously, when the missiles start flying, you can't call together a discussion group, but you'll be in a lot better shape if everything is working right and all your people are used to working as a close-knit team. Before taking off, a pilot flying a bombing mission will be much more prepared if he has been exposed to warlike conditions in training exercises and has talked with his teammates about the fear he has felt. I noticed that the commanders of the U.S. armed forces took a decidedly new approach to management during the Persian Gulf war. Instead of barking out orders, the commanding officers held team meetings on the front lines, and before going into battle, they talked with their soldiers about what to expect and how to help one another on the battlefield. That reassured me that the military really does endorse these ideas.

I was tremendously impressed by a recent commencement

speech given by retired Lieutenant General Melvin Zais at the Armed Forces Staff College. Zais shared with the graduates the one piece of advice he thought would advance their careers faster than anything: that they should care for their troops. He said, "It's got to bother you in your belly when you walk down the line of [soldiers] sitting under the wing of a plane or sitting near a chopper and they're loaded and the sweat's coming down their faces and they're really scared and you can smell it in their breath. And I can tell you, you can smell fear in a man's breath, but you'll never know it unless you get close enough to him to smell it. And if that bothers you, and you try to help him, you care." Zais concluded, "You cannot expect a soldier to be a proud soldier if you humiliate him. You cannot expect him to be brave if you abuse and cower him. You cannot expect him to be strong if you break him. . . . I enjoin you to be ever alert to the pitfalls of too much authority. Beware that you do not fall into the category of the little man with a little job and a big head. In essence, be considerate, treat your subordinates right, and they will literally die for you."

Zais was absolutely right. In fact, the whole Defense Department could benefit from the ideas behind participative management. Shortly after President Bush was elected, I talked with him about using PM and teamwork in the armed forces. Using the chimney metaphor, I described how people in various functions at Ford and other companies — marketing, finance, manufacturing, and so on — seldom share ideas with one another unless someone changes the system. The president-elect responded enthusiastically to the mental image of all those chimneys, saying that it described the Defense Department and the U.S. military to a T. Each branch of the military — the air force, the army, the marines, and the navy

— has its own chief of staff sitting on top of the chimney, and the only time that problem-solving discussions had taken place between the tops of the chimneys was when the Joint Chiefs of Staff got together. By the time an issue gets to the point where the top people become involved, of course, everyone is so locked into his position that it's difficult to change anything. So much work has gone into doing things the "army way," for instance, that the army chief of staff tends to take the tack that if he doesn't fight for the army's position, he won't be backing his troops. When people are put in that position, there's very little opportunity for compromise.

The president-elect and I talked about a way to make cross-chimney meetings happen far down in the hierarchy. I expressed my opinion that this could be very helpful. Since the four branches of the military have many problems in common, they might be able to cut their costs and improve quality dramatically if they got together to discuss those problems routinely at a lower level.

The Defense Department could definitely benefit from a quality improvement program to clean up its purchasing process and cut down on its bureaucracy and paperwork. At present, the Pentagon buys a lot of custom-made supplies and components. The military decides on an extremely detailed set of specifications for everything from the rivets in a ship to the toilet seats in a fighter jet. Then the Pentagon orders the product from a defense contractor or another firm that has been cleared to do military work, and gives that company the specifications so that everything is done the military way.

The Pentagon also doesn't trust anybody. When you're a defense contractor, you have to keep a detailed record of every hour a worker spends on a given job. Inspectors come into the company to verify that you're adhering to the military's pages of rules and specifications. If the Pentagon spots any sloppiness in your records, it throws the book at you; it might even hit you with a multimillion-dollar penalty, or a criminal one. In our nonmilitary work at Ford, we would never dream of doing something like that. I made a big push at Ford to eliminate time clocks altogether, because to me they're clear evidence of a lack of trust.

The military could cut down on waste by buying a lot more off-the-shelf commercial products, a step that was recommended several years ago in a study by the Packard Commission. There's absolutely no reason for the Pentagon to order custom-made parts when it can purchase products from a quality-minded commercial firm or even the corner hardware store.

One heartening development is the Defense Department's National Total Quality Management Symposium, which brings together government and industry leaders to talk about quality. The first one, hosted by Martin Marietta Corporation in 1989, drew more than nine hundred people; the second, hosted by Westinghouse in late 1990, was also a resounding success. The 1991 symposium, at which I have been invited to speak, is hosted by Boeing, and the keynote speaker is Boeing's CEO, Frank Shrontz. I'm pleased to see not only that the Defense Department is trying to adopt TQM but that it is working closely with industry to make continuous and lasting improvements.

Team Schools

We have to change the way we educate our kids. It's strange how our society works. We pit one child against another from kindergarten through the twelfth grade, and beyond. Our students study alone and they're graded as individuals; if we catch them working together, we consider it cheating. Then, after they graduate from high school or college and go to work, they're asked to quit competing with one another and begin cooperating, and perhaps to join coworkers on a company team.

These days, Ford and other companies need workers who can interact easily and share their knowledge to solve problems. It's not like the old days, when a person did one isolated job in his or her own world. Now jobs are closely interrelated. Manufacturing technicians often have to work together in order to keep very sophisticated equipment functioning, or they have to meet in teams with engineers to tackle a complicated problem.

School systems have developed a much bigger bureaucracy than is necessary, in much the same way that big companies have. There is also not nearly enough delegation of authority to the teachers or the principals running the schools. Teachers work in isolation. They get marching orders from the principals on what they must or must not include in the curriculum, and there's often no serious interaction between the math teacher and the English teacher, or the science teacher and the history teacher. Somehow we have to find ways to give each school more independence and let it do what is best for its students and teachers. If we can do that, we can start to use participative management and teamwork and have the teachers help the principal and other administrators come up with strategies to improve the schools.

We also need to make many structural changes and set goals for improvements. (The Bush administration appears to be doing this rather well.) The schools might make great strides if students began to work in teams early on in life. There is a small but growing interest in this approach. For example, a math teacher in Bakersfield, California, organizes his students in teams and assigns one of his best students to each team to help the others along. That school also gives its teachers a lighter-than-usual teaching load, so they have time to get together in teams to talk about students' needs and any problems they're having in their classrooms. The school has also brought parents into the teams to share ideas and to help the teachers learn more about the students.

In Rochester, New York, two old adversaries, the teachers' union chief and the superintendent of schools, have formed a partnership to restructure the district's sixty schools. That reminds me a bit of the cooperative relationship I had with Don Ephlin, the United Auto Workers leader at Ford. The Rochester program started with goal-setting. The partners determined what all students should know by the time they graduate from high school, and they came up with new ways of measuring student progress. Perhaps most important, administrators agreed to push decision-making down to the individual schools. Teachers have been given considerably more authority — and a 45 percent increase in pay over three years. That's what you call rewarding the people doing the actual work. In addition, all first-year teachers are supervised and trained by senior teachers, or mentors, and the school district and the union agreed on a rigorous system that makes sure the teachers are getting results. As the Rochester experience indicates, we could do a lot to improve the way our schools are managed.

Finally, we should lessen the emphasis on grades and search for a better way to measure the progress made by our children. Today's students tend to get caught up in trying to get an A or a B or in outperforming the rest of the class, neither of which necessarily means that they really know a subject. Perhaps grades should be replaced with more in-depth evaluations every year or so. I don't mean we should give the students one big multiple-choice test. The evaluation probably should be based on written essays or oral examinations, both proven methods for determining what individuals really know. Maybe then we would find out whether the teaching process is generating lasting results.

At the university level, I know of at least two schools that are trying to adopt total quality management. Michigan Tech, which is being helped along by Dan Rivard, an executive at Ford, and Oregon State University in Corvallis, Oregon, headed by John Byrne, are both looking for ways to run a truly high-quality university by using the basic principles we used at Ford. One classic problem in higher education is the adversarial relationship between very individualistic professors and the administrative staff. Universities could take some steps to alleviate that problem by getting their teaching staff and administrators to work in teams. I'm hoping that Michigan Tech and Oregon State will set the example in that area. A few success stories could work wonders.

The University of Washington has another good idea. It is changing its approach to engineering by showing students at the outset the real engineering applications of the skills they learn in difficult courses in science and math. Imagine having a professor teach you how something as arcane as calculus can be used in designing products. It's important for people to know how the work they're doing relates to the final product, and the students at Washington will be getting a dose of that. Also, by working in teams, they might even dream up products as a group, using calculus and physics to put them together. The University of Washington's effort is being undertaken in cooperation with six other schools, and another group of colleges is doing similar work.

Embracing the Philosophy Everywhere

Almost every time I pick up a newspaper, turn on the television, or walk into a store, I look for signs that people are putting the ideas I'm writing about to work. In fact, once you're tuned into this philosophy, it pretty much stays with you everywhere you go. I was at Loew's Ventana Canyon Resort in Tucson recently. The manager, Johnny So, obviously runs the place in a participative fashion. It's clear that all the people who work there love the man. I never sensed even one ounce of tentativeness when I asked an employee a question. I could tell that they have the flexibility to deal with problems in whatever way they think is right, and that's something I've developed a feeling for.

If you asked Johnny So whether he uses employee involvement, participative management, or teamwork, he'd probably tell you that he doesn't know what you're talking about. But it doesn't matter whether he calls it anything at all; the point is he's doing it, day in and day out. He's always out walking around and doing what he can to help. He's as much a part of the team as anyone.

I've also seen these ideas at work at a McDonald's restaurant. The workers were laughing and chattering, and it was a pleasant, upbeat place. I noticed that the manager was taking part in the work, doing whatever was needed at the moment, yet he was still keeping a close eye on how long customers were having to wait. It didn't bother him to pick up a half-empty box of fries and throw them away or to clean up some trays. The whole atmosphere was positive, and the place was clean as the dickens. Not long after that, I walked into another McDonald's, which was dirty and where the employees all seemed to have sour dispositions. The manager of that restaurant was standing in the back, just watching people work. Clearly, that boss was doing all the wrong things.

If I ever became the manager of a McDonald's, I'd start out by talking a lot with the employees. I would tell them how important it was that our team be customer-driven, and I'd point out that even though many of our customers were just passing through, we would also be serving a good number of regulars. I'd tell them, "If we serve them well, we'll keep our customers and our jobs, and we might even enjoy doing it." Then I'd encourage everyone to talk about their different jobs and tasks. "What's working and what isn't? Would it help if we learned one another's jobs? Is there anything I can do to make your job easier?" I'd look for ways to involve the employees in the decision-making. I might even get some of them involved in a little competitive benchmarking by giving them money to eat lunch at a Wendy's or a Burger King down the street, then asking them to tell the group what our rivals were up to. Why not? I know it's just a small restaurant, but even those little team activities could boost a worker's morale and self-esteem. In that sort of setting, there's enormous room for positive reinforcement.

Peter Ochs, a homebuilder in southern California, epitomizes what you can accomplish in a medium-size business. Ochs was named builder of the year in 1990 by *Professional Builder* magazine, and his company, Fieldstone, grew from a few million dollars in sales in 1981 to more than $368 million in 1990. Everything Ochs does, from monitoring the quality of his lumber to forming teams at the construction sites, is based on treating people with integrity and trust. He says the key to his success has been allowing people to "do all they're capable of doing, and creating an environment to allow that to happen." All of Fieldstone's employees take two courses sometime in their first year, one of them on managing interpersonal relations and the other on team problem-solving. That's the kind of training that I hope will be used throughout this country.

I've also noticed that some great athletes seem to agree. In a recent *Sports Illustrated* article, former New York Jets quarterback Joe Namath described how important it was, when he was out on the field and calling the plays, to tap the expertise of his teammates in the huddle. "A lot of what I called [when the Jets won the Superbowl] was 'check with me,' which meant I made the call at the line. I'd come back to the huddle and talk to Schmitty [John Schmitt], our center, or Haystack Herman, who was the tackle in front of Bubba Smith that day, and say, 'What do you like, Stack?' He'd say, 'Run a draw, Joe,' or 'We can trap him,' and I'd say, 'Okay, you got it.' "

The point, of course, is that a quarterback who makes the calls is a quarterback who can win the game. One who constantly has to look to the coach for instructions is trouble for the team. He'll be tentative, and his mind won't be on the actual play of the game, as Namath's was. That doesn't mean that a coach can't help call the plays, but the quarterback, who's tapping ideas from his teammates on the field, has to be the one in charge. Magic Johnson of the Los Angeles Lakers heaped praise on his new coach, Mike Dunleavy, when he told *Sports Illustrated,* "A lot of times, [Mike] will say, 'I'm not out there, what do you think?' . . . He remembers what it was like to play, and that's how he coaches." That definitely reinforces what I believe. Can you imagine having someone as talented as Magic on your team and not asking him, "What do you think?"

Taking These Ideas Home

As individuals, we can learn that embracing these ideas will help us in our daily lives. We can make life so much more enjoyable by going out of our way to appreciate all the little things that others do for us. It may sound simplistic, but it's enormously important to recognize and respect every human being. You'll be surprised by how much better you'll feel, and you'll get a lot more satisfaction out of life.

The people I genuinely admire build their relationships on trust. They're inherently positive, and acknowledge each person's importance in the world. My wife, Jody, is like that. She wouldn't think of hurting someone, and she treats people with respect no matter what position they hold. When people have a negative attitude, they wonder all the time why their lives are so lousy. They can't understand why people seem to be acting badly toward them. Basically, I think they'd feel much better about themselves if they followed the Golden Rule and treated others the way they would like to be treated.

If you think the ideas in this book make sense, you might want to try applying them in your personal life, not just on the job. You can't be a kind and considerate manager in the office and an angry bear at home — or vice versa. In fact, your entire family can benefit from these ideas. Whenever there's a lot of tension in a family, it's a pretty fair guess that somebody has a negative attitude that makes it tough for people to get along.

Parents often don't give their kids enough freedom to make their own choices. I'm not advocating indiscriminate permissiveness, but you can be a responsible parent and still find ways to empower your children to make decisions on their own, which will build their self-confidence. It's also important to learn how to communicate, especially to listen to them and not reject everything they say. If you come down hard every time one of your kids raises an idea, you're probably the person creating the bad atmosphere.

Almost anyone can change his attitude if he works at it. Jack Telnack, the design genius behind the Taurus, spent his early years in a design center where one person was often pitted against another, which created some pretty fierce rivalries. Jack was undoubtedly affected by that, so he naturally had some trouble shifting gears. In the early 1980s, I asked a man named Don Kopka, who was a real team player, to try to change the atmosphere in the design center. He and Jack talked about the past and discussed ways in which Jack and the other designers might work better as a team. It took awhile, but as Jack gradually came to trust Don, they began to cooperate. The cooperation between the two leaders then spread throughout the design center.

A great many people tend to mellow as they get older, too. From what I hear about the old days, Henry Ford II was much more understanding in his later years than in his early ones. During the years that I knew him well, he certainly treated people considerately. When Henry came to our worldwide management conference in 1984 and introduced our mission, values, and guiding principles statement he must have been saying that he saw merit in the ideas it expressed. And he let me know that he liked the improvements he saw in the way people at the company interacted.

That reassured me that we had made a change for the better.

Causes for Concern

14

Dealing with Japan

The United States has to do something about Japan before it's too late. We have to realize that even if U.S. companies could put in place everything I've talked about in this book and dramatically improve quality, they could still be in trouble, because Japan plays by a different set of trade and economic rules from the ones Americans use. Japan's rules have served that country well in achieving its goal of economic dominance.

Japan's view of the world was captured remarkably well by the popular historian Barbara Tuchman in a 1936 article in *Foreign Affairs* magazine: "Unlike an individual, a nation cannot admit itself in error; so Japan's only answer has been to tell herself that her judges are wrong and she is right. To strengthen this contention she has built up the belief that she acts from the purest motives, which her fellow nations willfully misunderstand. The more they disapprove, the more adamant grows Japan's conviction that she is right. . . . So completely divorced is that Japanese mental process from the Occidental, so devoid of what Westerners call logic, that the

Japanese are able to make statements, knowing they present a false picture, yet sincerely believing them."

That seems as true now as it was over fifty years ago. Even today, it would be futile for us to try to persuade the Japanese that their approach to trade and economic matters is wrong and that they should follow American practices. They *believe* in their approach, whether or not it is objectively wrong or right. The Japanese way of handling these issues is grounded in their tradition, and they hold on to that way because it is beneficial to their country.

The Japanese have also figured out how to use U.S. laws on imports and customs regulations, as well as our political system, to their own advantage. They have discovered that any action that our government takes against them can be made to backfire, and their hired lobbyists have learned how to make full use of the openness of our political process. For instance, some members of Congress recently tried to ban sales of Toshiba products in the United States because the Japanese giant sold top-secret submarine technology to the Soviets. But lobbyists hired by Toshiba pointed out that U.S. computer makers would suffer if Congress cut off their supplies of Toshiba's computer chips. When the computer makers heard this, they put additional pressure on Congress not to punish the Japanese corporation, which is one of their most reliable suppliers. In the end, all Toshiba got was a slap on the wrist.

A lot of things the Japanese have been doing lately bother me. For example, whenever we try to talk to them about trade or aid to developing countries, they seem reluctant to cooperate. They also appear uncomfortable when we ask them to join us in a joint military action, such as fighting the war in the Persian Gulf. However, the Japanese are confident and aggressive when they act alone. Recently, leading Japanese politicians such as Shintaro Ishihara have taken every opportunity to portray the United States as a nation of racists, yet by every measure the Japanese have a problem much like our own. Koreans in Japan are treated like various minority groups have historically been treated here. And Japanese-owned factories in the United States have a poor track record in granting equal opportunity to women, African-Americans, and other minorities. The Japanese purposely open new factories in non-union areas away from Detroit and other major cities, and all employees are carefully screened to determine their social and political thinking. And rarely do the Japanese put Americans in positions of any real power or responsibility.

One Door Is Open, Another Door Closed

Over the past ten years, Japan's share of the U.S. automotive market has climbed from the high teens to nearly 30 percent of all cars sold. Most of our attention has been on imports of Japanese cars, but statistics that focus on fully assembled imports are missing the main point. The real growth in Japan's share of the U.S. market lies in the two million vehicles the Japanese are assembling each year at their American plants. The vast majority of the parts in those cars and trucks come from Japan, but by appearing to show restraint on their car exports, the Japanese have built good will. Simultaneously, when they came here, they made a big show of opening new plants and creating jobs, contrasting themselves with the American automakers, who, in their alleged weakness, have been cutting back employment.

Our members of Congress and governors have been getting an earful from concerned business leaders about Japan's invasion, but politicians are generally welcoming the Japanese with open arms. Governors visit Japan frequently to lobby for their investments, as do mayors from our major cities. This seems to me like a pretty serious mistake, because the Japanese are gaining more and more control of our economic destiny. They say that they're using American-made parts to build their cars here, but they're not, and that's hurting many small U.S. companies. The Japanese automakers buy all the critically important parts, such as engines and electronic components, from Japanese suppliers, and any state-of-the-art technology almost always comes directly from Japan. The U.S. Customs Service is supposed to keep track of what they are importing, but the laws and inspections are highly subjective, and there are various ways to disguise the imports from another country. Again, this behavior makes sense to the Japanese because it benefits their country.

American automakers essentially have no presence in Japan. It's a long, sad story. Long before World War II, the original Henry Ford bought property in Yokohama Bay. Ford owned that property, with one interruption when it was confiscated during the war, until the 1970s. Mr. Ford always wanted to start up an assembly plant and gradually develop it into a full manufacturing facility, but the Japanese government wouldn't let him. There was only one brief span when we could have started a plant there — during the U.S. occupation of Japan after the war — but the company couldn't afford it at the time. The minute General Douglas MacArthur moved out of Japan, the Japanese government decided to protect Japanese industries by blocking all foreign investments.

As Japan got stronger, its government eliminated many of the laws against foreign investment, but it resorted to a highly developed system of impediments that still make it very difficult for Americans to export products to Japan or set up facilities there. The Japanese can point to IBM Japan, Fuji Xerox, and other joint ventures that are successful. But the fact is that we just don't have a U.S.-owned manufacturing presence in Japan, as we do in other countries. The Japanese argue that we give up too easily and that we're not willing to learn their ways. There are elements of truth in that, but their market is most definitely closed. If the market were open, I would have succeeded in my effort to build an American car compatible in all ways with the Japanese market, with the steering wheel on the right side and all, and exported it to Japan. If that market were open, our planners would have found a way to accommodate my desire. For much of the 1970s and 1980s, there was no way to slice through all the paperwork. Each and every car had to go through a maze of approvals. In Japan, you have to sell cars door to door. But our salespeople wound up sitting around the import authority office waiting for permission to bring their cars in. The officials were extremely adept at being out to lunch or taking a tea break. Days could go by, and a salesman who is stuck at the import office isn't selling any cars.

It's no mystery that the Japanese keep out products and companies that they perceive to be threats to their economy. They're not worried about fast-food restaurants, so the restaurants get in, but most of them are just franchises. Automobiles are too important to be allowed to penetrate. The Japanese wouldn't dream of letting a major industry such as automobiles be diminished from 90 percent to 65 percent of their market, but that's what Americans did. And we're talking about a vital industry that accounts for two of the three largest American companies, General Motors and Ford, plus a large network of suppliers.

Uncle Sam Is Just Sitting on His Hands

As a nation, we can't seem to take a strong position on trade with Japan. I'm not sure why. I think the unending flow of sophisticated intellectual thought from American economists about the purity of "free trade," and the contempt they have had for anything else over the years, has scared off even the strongest of presidents and other leaders. I can't think of any president who has been willing to tell Japan's leadership bluntly that we can no longer tolerate the huge trade imbalance between our two countries. What if we had a president who met with Japan's leaders and said that things must change? Instead, recent presidents have told Japan's prime ministers, "Don't worry. We're a free-trade country." After the Japanese leaders hear that, it's useless for business leaders to try to convince the heads of Japanese companies that something has to be done about the trade imbalance.

Instead of criticizing Japan's approach to trade, we criticize ourselves, almost as if we have a need to take ourselves to task. The Japanese have succeeded in making us all believe that our trade problems are the result of a fundamental weakness that makes us incapable of producing quality goods and services. I still find myself in conversations with U.S. leaders who repeat the broad-brush cliché about the weakness of American business. They'll ask me, "Why can't we buckle down and compete with the Japanese instead of doing all this crying and complaining?" If our government helps

American firms, they say, businesses will get lazy and the quality of U.S. products will decline. Japanese companies became strong while their government assisted them and protected their home market from foreign competition. According to conventional wisdom, they should have remained weak.

I'm not suggesting that our government close our borders to products from Japan or any other country. Our standard of living has improved significantly because of the growth in international trade. Taking extreme action against a huge trader such as Japan would be the worst thing in the world. But having watched how Japan operates, I'd say, "Okay, you've shown you know how to work your system. You decide the best way to bring things into balance. It's probably a whole mixture of things, but you simply must change. You must correct the problem."

We should not let ourselves get drawn into endless debates with the Japanese over specifics, such as the dispute over how much American beef Japan should buy. Japanese trade representatives dance us dizzy when we try to debate them issue by issue. Part of what they know is that our trade representatives and other officials keep on changing, so we hardly ever have people with long-term experience negotiating on our behalf. And we have so few people with any real understanding of the Japanese language or of Japanese culture. In contrast, Japan's representatives are skilled veterans who know every trick in the book.

When it comes to tackling these issues, we need to follow a policy that protects our national interest, just as other countries protect theirs. We're now facing a Europe that puts Europe's concerns first, just as Japan puts Japan's concerns first. Yet we can't even have a reasonable debate about what our policies should be in the United States without raising cries of protectionism. At some point, we have to accept the differences among countries and develop a plan that is going to benefit the interests of the United States as well as foster international trade. If we don't, our position in the world will decline faster than we expect.

Europe's Battle Against Japan, Inc.

Many European CEOs and politicians are worried about competition from the Japanese, but some of them have a touch of arrogance. They talk about Japan in much the same way the CEOs in the U.S. computer and electronics industry did a decade ago when they said, "If those of you in the Rust Belt managed your companies well, then you wouldn't have any problem." I'm sure they thought we looked weak and paralyzed by fear. Right now, some Europeans are talking the same game.

Up to this point, the governments of the European countries have done more to protect their companies from the Japanese than our government has. Former British Prime Minister Margaret Thatcher reached a quiet agreement with the Japanese that their share of Britain's automotive market would not go any higher than 11.5 percent. This was not published officially, but it was widely understood in the industry. Other European countries have similar quotas. Frankly, I wouldn't blame the European Community if it imposed a community-wide quota system to prevent the Japanese from increasing their market share beyond a set limit in Europe. The EC could also avoid what happened among suppliers in America by requiring the Japanese to use a certain percentage of European parts in the cars they produce in Europe.

The Europeans, particularly the Germans, are actually outstanding role models for how to compete worldwide. They are aggressive, but they are also fair. Unlike the Japanese, the Germans have allowed foreign competitors to participate fully in their home market. And when they open a plant or facility in the United States, they hire Americans to run it, unlike the Japanese, who keep their own people at the top of their operations no matter where they're located. German firms with U.S. plants also rely on American suppliers for many of their parts and components. Americans have considerably less trouble doing business with the Europeans, because they play by a set of rules that are similar to ours.

The Truth — or Bear the Consequences

One of the most striking things about the Japanese in wartime was the fanaticism with which they fought and their belief that defeat was simply unacceptable. They demonstrate that same single-mindedness in peacetime. No matter what industry they enter, their goal is total dominance. As a result of their aggressiveness, the American steel industry has been devastated, and most of our firms that produce machine tools have withered away, especially the ones that make cutting-edge equipment. The American consumer electronics industry is almost completely gone: no U.S. company makes VCRs or compact disc players, and the number of television makers in this country has dropped from twenty-six to one: Zenith.

If the United States does not do something to curtail Japan's expansion into our automotive market, by the end of the decade the Japanese will have increased their share from

30 percent to as much as 40 percent. The Europeans have already lost most of the market share that they're going to lose, so American companies will continue to lose market share. I suppose that the Japanese do have some kind of limit in their minds, and that they realize that if they go beyond a certain point, they'll risk killing the goose that lays all the golden eggs. But I wouldn't bet that they've reached the limit yet.

Japan has also infiltrated the technological levels of the American industrial base. Almost 90 percent of our state-of-the-art memory chips are made in Japan. Not only does Japan's control of these chips, which are the building blocks of all electronic devices, pose a threat to us, but U.S. computer makers face quite a challenge competing with companies that make all their own chips at a significantly lower cost than what we pay for them. Over time, Japan could leverage its technological strength and cost advantages to take over a large share of the American computer industry. Though computers are not my field of expertise, it seems to me that unless the Japanese slow down, our computer makers will find it almost impossible to keep pace. And if Japan ultimately controls the hardware, it will certainly be able to slash our lead in computer software. Imagine what would happen if Microsoft's Bill Gates, the young genius behind the software that runs the IBM PC, had to design his programs for Japanese-made computers. He would have an obvious disadvantage compared to Japanese software developers, who already have close relationships with their country's computer firms.

Unless your technical people are involved in making products, their skill and expertise wither, and most of the high-paying, rewarding work moves overseas. I think that in altogether too many technical areas, the Japanese still have a dramatic advantage over the United States. That places American firms in real jeopardy. Knowledgeable people who aren't worried about our future baffle me.

Having virtually eliminated our consumer electronics industry, the Japanese also have an extraordinary advantage in a blossoming field called high-definition television. Known as HDTV, this technology gives a TV screen the crystal-clear sharpness of a 35mm photograph. Experts believe that millions of us will soon trade in our conventional TVs for HDTVs, and the vast majority of the new models will be Japanese-made. Now that the Japanese control the electronic equipment used by consumers and the electronic media, they're moving to become the primary provider of the programs the equipment carries. That's why they are buying Hollywood studios and record companies. In the past five years, Sony bought Columbia Pictures and CBS Records, and Matsushita acquired MCA, a giant in TV programming, in 1991. The Japanese objective is clear: they want to control every segment of the consumer electronics industry, from microchip to broadcasting.

Japan's dominance in that industry gives them advantages in other areas as well. At Ford, we saw this firsthand. Consumer electronics giants such as Matsushita, Sony, and JVC are working closely with Japanese automakers and letting them know well in advance about the hottest new stereo gadgets, so the automakers can include them in their cars and trucks. While the Japanese manufacturers were installing the latest equipment, very often what we were offered were earlier generations of the technology. That's why Ford decided to continue making its own radios and other audio equipment and made a broad effort to build a core base of knowledge in the entire electronics area. The average Ford car or truck contains more than $1,200 in electronic equipment, and cars use electronics to control steering, braking, the engine, the transmission, the suspension, and so on. If we depended on the Japanese to provide us with the technology, we would almost always be a generation or two behind.

The challenge we face in competing with Japan is one of our toughest, but it's not an impossible battle. The first step is to get over thinking about whether Japan's behavior is necessarily right or wrong and to recognize that that's the way the world is. The sooner we do this, the sooner we'll be able to act forcefully and aggressively to maintain our place in the world economy.

15

Honing the Competitive Edge

Early in 1991, *Forbes* reporter Jerry Flint wrote an article about me that focused on the decline of America's manufacturing base. The accompanying photograph was sort of amusing. There I was, sitting all alone on the longest park bench you ever saw, still dressed in suit and tie as if I had somewhere to go. But the text (and the text of many of my speeches these days) focused on one of my main preoccupations. In the article, I pointed out how critically important manufacturing is to the nation's economy and said that we have to find a way of stopping its continuing erosion. When I raise this concern, most people tell me not to worry about it; they tell me that America is simply switching from a manufacturing economy to a service-based economy, just as we moved from agriculture to manufacturing early in our history.

We certainly should do everything we can to help our service industries thrive and become global leaders, but I strongly disagree that our problems in manufacturing and the related drop in our technical prowess are nothing to worry about. I can't think of a single great world power since the industrial revolution that didn't have a strong manufacturing base. The United States is still a great military power, but our industrial base is crumbling before our eyes. Not long ago, this country was active in almost every aspect of technology. We made all the key components that went into computers, cars, televisions, and other goods. Now we're hardly active in a growing number of areas, not just consumer electronics. Today, in many industries we build nothing more than the outer shell of a product, which means we are the assemblers of parts made overseas. If you look inside the original IBM Personal Computer and virtually all PCs that are now available, you'll see that almost everything was made in Asia.

Some people think I'm overly pessimistic. They point to the 1980s as the nation's longest sustained economic boom since World War II. That may be true, but we funded that growth period by going into massive debt. While times seemed good in the '80s, thousands of jobs moved overseas, and a close look at the statistics shows that many of the high-income jobs that led our society to the top are disappearing, because we're making fewer and fewer of the products that provide those high-paying jobs.

If we allow this slide in our manufacturing base to continue, and naively believe that the service sector can provide jobs for everyone, the United States will lose its position of preeminence and become an also-ran. Why should we care? On a personal level, our standard of living will decline, both in absolute terms and relative to that of people in other countries. Even now, it often takes the income of two adults to provide the lifestyle we've come to expect. It's no accident that the acronym DINC (double income, no children) is coming into common usage. In the future, we will have to work more and will be able to buy less, while the prosperity of people in other countries will continue to climb. Anyone who has traveled to Europe or Japan recently understands what I am saying. As the dollar becomes progressively less valuable than it once was relative to foreign currencies, the ease with which Americans have traveled the world for so long will steadily decline.

Retaining our preeminence in the world also matters because the American concepts of freedom and fair play are the best that any society has developed, and the world will benefit if the United States remains a role model for developing countries. A disturbing number of them no longer look at the United States that way. I am almost certain that every nation in Asia has shifted its focus from America to Japan; for the foreseeable future, we should assume that countries such as South Korea, Thailand, and Singapore will behave more like Japan than the United States, particularly in trade matters and economic policies. And I'm also sure that the Eastern European countries are modeling themselves on Germany, not the United States. As long as the United States was seen as the world leader in economic performance, developing countries could believe that it was possible both to improve economically and to improve the treatment and standard of living of their people, even though that meant substantial increases in social, environmental, and safety costs. Now I believe they are beginning to question that assumption.

How did the United States lose its stature? From World War II to 1980, American companies not only had our home market almost totally to ourselves, but we enjoyed similar advantages and success in foreign markets. We lulled ourselves into thinking that our research and engineering was good enough and our manufacturing capabilities were perfectly okay. In fact, for a number of years the United States did have a major technological edge over the rest of the world, because we had such a huge lead in the late 1940s. The people running our companies put their best employees in the finance and marketing departments, thinking that the key to being successful was to have the best cost controls and to do the best marketing and selling job. As a result, the people who took charge at a lot of companies were the aggressive financial and marketing brains. But ignoring engineering and manufacturing wasn't our only mistake. We also neglected to spend the money needed to develop some great research and technical know-how into products that had special appeal to customers. For instance, the videocassette recorder was invented here, but the Japanese were the ones who ended up manufacturing it in mass quantities, virtually cornering the world market for VCRs.

Whenever you're trying to develop new products, there's always a point when you either have to fish or cut bait. You can continue to play around with the technology in a research stage, or you can spend some serious money and get on with it. In too many cases in the past several decades, the people who ran U.S. companies failed to take the risks and spend the money necessary to offer new products.

Most companies are managed in a way that tends to discourage people from taking a risk. If someone pushes ahead, tries something, and fails, he is sure to hear about it. But if a manager avoids taking a risk that should be taken, it tends to go unnoticed and his reputation remains unblemished, because the cost of a lost opportunity rarely gets recorded. I call these errors of omission because they involve not doing something that would have been worthwhile. They are a pervasive and destructive element at many companies, and often determine whether a company lives or dies.

To counteract the tendency to avoid risk, companies need

to foster an environment that encourages people to take the initiative in seeking out better ways of designing and manufacturing old products and introducing a steady stream of new products. If American managers had done this in the past, the natural desire of people to do a better job would have emerged, and this country would be much further ahead of where it is right now. If the people at lower levels who knew the technology had been empowered to make more decisions, the real visionaries — maybe the individuals who invented the technology — would have been heard by the decision-makers who had the money to spend. We would have been able to remain in many of the markets we abandoned, and if we had continuously improved the products for those markets, nobody would have been able to touch the United States.

Still Playing Catch-up

A number of U.S. firms would make most people's lists of the companies that have improved most over the past decade or so; Motorola, Xerox, Merck, Milliken, Rubbermaid, Sara Lee, Hewlett-Packard, and Ford are a few examples. Having been aroused by foreign competition, these companies have improved their quality and are holding their own or even gaining in world market share. It's refreshing to see that the organizations doing all this hard work are beginning to reap some benefits from it.

In the service sector of the economy, Federal Express seems to be as good as anyone. It has a great system in place that routes all the packages through a Memphis hub, allowing the company to guarantee on-time, error-free deliveries. Federal

Express has also given its employees a lot of authority to make decisions. Nordstrom department store is another top-notch operation that puts a great deal of power in the hands of its workers, especially the local store managers and sales-people. But these companies are exceptions, not the rule. Many companies are still having trouble with quality, and one of the major reasons is that they don't have a participa-tive approach to management. I can sense that's true when I hear lower-level managers talk about what's going on. Re-cently, I heard one of them say that managers in his company have "lively discussions — until we get our instructions from upper management."

Companies often pay lip service to the ideas of teamwork and participative management, but they cling to the old top-down method of managing. To them, asking workers what they think is all just a waste of time and an exercise that won't really change anything. What they are missing is the energiz-ing effect of involving employees more in the decision-making process. The flow of ideas and information increases, and the person making the decision is better informed. Companies that don't accept this, even if they're among the best U.S. firms, might have a difficult time when they encounter for-eign competitors.

I expressed my thoughts about this recently at Boeing, which makes more than half of the world's commercial air-craft and is America's biggest exporter. Frank Shrontz, its CEO, is a powerful advocate of quality excellence. Boeing has some tough domestic competitors, such as McDonnell Doug-las and Lockheed, but its only sizable foreign rival is Europe's Airbus Industries. I suggested that a good strategy for Boeing would be to assume that the Japanese are planning to move eventually into the commercial aircraft business as a competitor. They'll probably start in Japan and then expand into Asian markets. Their ultimate goal will probably be to reduce Boeing's market share to 25 to 30 percent, or less than half of what it enjoys now. Later that same day, a Boeing vice president told me that Toyota had just announced its plans to manufacture small planes. That's step one.

Making Competitiveness a Priority

Even though the U.S. industrial base has lost substantial ground to foreign competitors and is far weaker than it was ten to fifteen years ago, no one in Washington is providing a vision of what we must do to improve our overall economic strength. We need a call to action, but I don't hear one, and I think we are floundering.

The president needs to call greater attention to the economic war we are fighting. We can't continue to attack a problem like this in a piecemeal way. The government must factor competitiveness into every action. Every law that is passed, every regulation that is issued, must be assessed to determine the effect it will have on our ability to compete. Right now, the economic health of our industrial sector is rarely a consideration in our government's decisions. Having traveled the world these past sixteen years, I have found that most countries' governments take the opposite approach. They automatically examine the consequences any government action will have on the country's ability to compete. They are also constantly looking for ways to help their companies compete in the global markets. Business leaders in these other countries have access to the top people in the government; helping business is part of the continuing dialogue. The contrast here in the United States is striking. We do now have a presidential council on competitiveness, headed by Vice President Dan Quayle, but I'm not aware of any strong actions it has taken.

Some people think the United States government should create a cabinet-level post, similar to Japan's minister of international trade and industry, to oversee competitive concerns. I don't endorse that, because the issues might get lost in the political shuffle of high-level debates. The president should take the lead and be the driving force behind making competitiveness a major issue. When he submits a budget, he should call attention to items that help companies compete, and when he meets with leaders from the Senate or the House, he should harp on competitiveness. If the president did that, the issue might become a primary concern each time the government considers taking an action.

I'm not expecting a lot of help in this area from Capitol Hill, however. Today, our representatives in Congress seem to skim the surface on most issues. Our legislative system has evolved in such a way that representatives are asked to make decisions on far too many subjects and often wind up taking actions based on superficial hallway briefings from bright young staffers as they are hurrying to a committee meeting for a vote. Staffers sometimes have so much influence over the actions taken by the members of Congress that our system, which is based on representation of the public interest, breaks down. A representative's vote becomes a reflection of the personal agenda of a staff person, who isn't answerable to the voting public.

Specific Action for Uncle Sam

The present administration also has to follow through completely on President Bush's pledge to be the "education president." The nation's public school system is not working well. About a third of our eighteen-year-olds are educational failures; they either dropped out of school or can barely read the diplomas given to them at graduation. Because of this, American companies wind up teaching thousands of their workers how to read and write. How can we remain a first-rate country if our workers can't read a manual or don't have the math background needed to apply statistics on the job?

I believe the Bush administration wants to pay serious attention to the problem. I was pleased when the president gathered the nation's governors for an education summit, during which they agreed to set specific national goals for all 16,000 school districts. And I think the country will make progress under the leadership of Lamar Alexander, who became secretary of education in mid-1991. Alexander proposed a plan that will create an experimental school in each of the 435 congressional districts, which will be used as models for the other schools in the districts. The plan also allows parents and students to choose which school children will attend. As schools compete for students, principals and teachers will be forced to improve the way they operate. I think Alexander will be supported by the business community, and I applaud him for appointing former Xerox CEO David T. Kearns as his deputy.

The government also has to take the lead in taming the soaring cost of health care. Every year Americans spend an average of $2,200 per person on health insurance, pharmaceuticals, and medical services, totaling more than 12 percent of our gross national product. American companies bear a good deal of that burden: Ford's health-care expenses add an average of $350 to the price of a Ford car, up from about $50 in 1970. It's hard to compete internationally when companies in countries such as Japan and Germany spend significantly less than that. If current trends continue, health-care spending soon will account for more than a quarter of our nation's GNP.

To deal with this, we should begin by assembling all the facts about our system and determine where costs are rising fastest and why. Someone, perhaps in the U.S. government, should also get the facts about the health-care systems in several key countries and evaluate them. Canada, Germany, and a third industrialized country are good candidates. Canadians, for instance, spend about 8.5 percent of their GNP on health care. Their system is more socialized than ours: rather than paying any out-of-pocket money for medical services, Canadian citizens have a health-care system that is entirely publicly funded; the government reimburses doctors, hospitals, and other professionals for their services. Canada and essentially all other countries place a cap on the total amount that is spent on health care. This means that everywhere but in the United States, health-care providers accept the idea that a limit will be placed on the total spending for medical services.

I'm not advocating that we copy some other country's health-care system, but we could certainly learn something by studying other ways of doing things. I also recognize that there are several powerful interests with different views concerning the way we approach health care. The professional health-care providers, the companies bearing the costs, the insurance firms, the pharmaceutical firms, the hospital supply firms, and the educational institutions all have strong stakes in this issue. But we've got to do something, because health-care spending is out of control, and it's definitely hurting our competitiveness. As it is, almost all of our energy and imagi-nation has gone into how we can shift the burden from one party to the next. We need to redirect that energy to find an affordable system that serves the needs of our society.

Congress and the White House should also continue to support changes in our antitrust laws that would permit not only precompetitive research but joint development of new technologies needed to meet future requirements. Past en-forcement of the antitrust laws has made the average Amer-ican executive gun-shy when it comes to extensive cooperative efforts. Under the auspices of the National Cooperative Re-search Act of 1984, however, U.S. automakers are now work-ing together to achieve technological breakthroughs in areas such as the increased use of plastics and other composites, as well as technologies to improve emissions. U.S. auto pro-ducers are also working with the oil industry to research cleaner-burning gasoline and other fuels. This cooperative trend should be encouraged and accelerated. In Japan, coop-eration in the national interest is more the norm, even though companies remain fiercely competitive with one another. The United States needs to find a way to permit and encourage that sort of cooperation in the national interest. I hope we are long past the days when it was widely believed that the auto and oil companies conspired to withhold major known fuel economy improvements because they would hurt oil industry profits. In today's competitive environment, that sort of im-agined conspiracy would be economic nonsense.

It goes without saying that our government needs to follow

fiscal policies that keep inflation and interest rates low. Even a small change in interest rates substantially affects the cost of building a new plant or buying industrial equipment. For much of the past twenty years, American companies were faced with competition from foreign companies, particularly from those based in Japan and Germany, that were able to borrow money at interest rates that were often 50 percent lower than ours. That began to change when the Federal Reserve trimmed rates in 1990 and 1991 to cope with the recession, but history indicates that we will again be at a disadvantage when the recession ends.

We could learn a lot by studying how the Japanese government helps its companies plan for the future by issuing white papers that identify specific industries and technologies for concentration and development. In the past, it has frequently given money, primarily for research, to a particular industry. I don't advocate U.S. government financial support for specific industries, but we should try to identify new technologies that will have a major impact on our economy, and provide incentives that will encourage companies in the private sector to put their energy into them. The National Science Foundation and the National Academies of Science and Engineering would be able to identify a dozen or more technologies that are going to be important in the future. I imagine the list would include high-definition television, superconductivity, biotechnology, and structural plastics.

What Companies Should Do

All American firms should make quality improvement their number-one priority. You can't begin to compete in the world markets unless your products or services are first-class and reasonably priced. Beyond improving quality, American firms can boost the nation's competitive strength by finding ways to keep manufacturing here at home. When a company moves a production operation overseas to Taiwan or Singapore, the short-term results can be good; that company's costs go down and its profits go up. But if too many American companies take that path, they will not only eliminate jobs here, they will weaken the nation's industrial base. In addition, companies that farm everything out lose touch with what's going on in the manufacturing arena, and soon their engineering and manufacturing people have less hands-on expertise, because the factories making their products are thousands of miles away.

I've talked a lot in this book about the importance of concurrent product development — getting teams of engineers, designers, and manufacturing people to work together. That gets mighty difficult when the manufacturing source is across the Pacific Ocean. I don't think you can keep your engineers on the cutting edge in that situation, because they don't have the critically important daily interaction with the manufacturing people. You will probably wind up moving some of your highly paid technical employees overseas to work at the production sites. In fact, I believe that has already happened, and the process is accelerating.

At Ford, we increased our purchase of foreign-made components when the Japanese yen was weak relative to the U.S. dollar. We even started to import core components such as automotive engines and transaxles. Fortunately, we realized that if we farmed out all of our engines and transaxles, we would lose important technical competence. We received a lot of cooperation from employees throughout the company and found ways to avoid shipping the work to Asia. Those "keep it home" strategies helped us improve our technical abilities throughout the 1980s, and enabled us to reestablish our strength in the middle of the automotive market.

Companies should also be continually scouring the globe for ideas. The benchmarking process, in which you find the world's best of each process and technology you use, can be very useful. Look for the best applications and ideas you can find and then adopt them if you can. You can achieve a remarkable number of improvements and cost savings by adopting techniques that someone else is already using.

Technical people like to write about what they're doing, and American managers have always paid close attention to all the English-language publications. But we haven't kept up to date on Japanese and other Asian journals the way we should. We should also be studying the features built into low-volume, high-priced products coming out of Japan and Europe. Often the very latest features are found initially only in the higher-priced models, because they are too expensive to be included in the mass-produced models. For example, state-of-the-art automotive features such as electronic air suspension and antilock braking systems showed up first in luxury cars. Once you spot a new feature, the trick is to figure out how to add it to your own products at a reasonable cost. Companies should also benchmark themselves. Some of the best ideas in the world might be sitting in your own research department.

I can't overemphasize the importance of hiring and promoting managers who are technically knowledgeable. Many Japanese CEOs and high-level managers have come up through the technical side of their companies, in engineering or manufacturing. Here we seem to think that it doesn't matter how much you know about the nuts and bolts of the business — that if you have the basic general management skills, you can run just about any company. The problem is that such managers lack the background to know when to take technical risks and frequently don't realize that they are missing major long-term opportunities for improvement.

Merck, the highly regarded drug maker, is a great role model for American companies in this area. Roy Vagelos, the company's CEO, is a trained physician and is extremely knowledgeable about pharmaceuticals. In fact, Roy spent a good part of his life working in and overseeing their research and development. He can readily tell when a scientist in the laboratory comes up with something good that the company should develop. The basic general manager might say, "That's very interesting, and I hope it works out," but he or she is not likely to take a proactive step. A manager who has come up through marketing might tell the researcher, "If you can ever make that work, I can sell it," but he or she might not know when to pour the financial and manpower resources into the new idea.

The American CEOs who have the most technical knowledge seem to be the heads of electronic corporations. The cofounders of Hewlett-Packard are both engineers, as is John Young, the current CEO. Ken Olsen, who founded and still runs Digital Equipment Corporation, is an engineer, and I can't think of one software company that isn't headed by someone who has an extensive knowledge of the software it's selling. But the old-line product manufacturing companies seem to be run by general managers who got their experience in marketing or finance or were brought in from another company. For some reason, the longer a company has been in business in this country, the less likely it seems to be that it will be headed by someone who knows the technical and operating side of the business.

Last, the United States as a whole has to make manufacturing products that will compete in the world's commercial markets at least as high a priority as building fighter jets and tanks. One of the reasons that the Japanese and Germans have surpassed us in many technical fields is that their best and brightest people are busy making products for average customers instead of working for defense firms. When Ford tries to hire graduates from the best universities, we often lose some of the top candidates to military giants such as Hughes Aircraft, General Dynamics, and Raytheon. Those firms look far more exciting to an engineer or a scientist than a U.S. automaker does. People tend to yawn at the idea of setting up new factories. And with our spectacular victory over Iraq in the Persian Gulf, I doubt that the fascination with military technology is going to diminish anytime soon.

But I haven't given up hope. Managers are beginning to focus more attention on engineering and manufacturing, and companies are developing a voracious demand for scientific and engineering competence. Because of this, technical training that includes engineering and manufacturing in addition to business is the "in" thing at Michigan, Stanford, the University of Washington, and a number of other schools. When students begin to see scientists and engineers being hired at good salaries by American manufacturing companies, they will recognize that a technical education holds a real future for them. Encouraging more young people to enter technical fields will help the United States avoid losing any more muscle from its industrial base.

The Need for Corporate — and Personal — Renewal

The entrepreneur, the individual who launches an entirely new company built on one idea, fortunately is still a strong phenomenon in American business, and entrepreneurs continually feed new products and services into the economy. A high percentage of the start-ups fail, but that's all right, because most of the innovators behind them are young, and they will try again. Those who succeed in a big way, such as Bill Gates at Microsoft, become almost national gurus. We should do everything we can to maintain the strength and vitality of this process in the United States.

Unfortunately, very few large companies maintain their entrepreneurial spirit and energy. They become stagnant, getting into a rut of doing things the same old way. Larger companies face the difficult task of renewing themselves continuously. One of the best times to do that is when a company changes its top management. A new person frequently comes in with a real burst of energy and a willingness to shake up the bureaucracy with new ideas and bold actions. That's why it seems dangerous to me for any CEO — or any manager — to stay in the same job for very long; I believe in the idea of "repotting" yourself by doing something new every five or ten years. That's the main reason I left Ford in 1990. In my last ten years there, first as president and COO and then as chairman and CEO, I pretty much accomplished all that I could in implementing my ideas for improvement.

While it's doubtful that the major long-term thrust of the company will change dramatically, because my successor, Red Poling, and I worked so closely together, Red will certainly put his own stamp on Ford. I also believe that the company will benefit when a new pair of executives take charge and promote their own ideas about the best game plan for the future. Ford's rival General Motors just changed its top management, when Bob Stempel replaced Roger Smith as CEO. Stempel will certainly be an agent for change; under him, GM is likely to take a path similar to the one Ford took, stressing teamwork and continuous improvement. In fact, one of Ed Deming's key disciples, Bill Scherkenbach, was hired away from Ford by General Motors.

If GM does change in this way, it will be of great competitive concern to Ford. When GM was banking more heavily on the magic of science and technology than on the people side of the business, as it did in the 1980s, I felt pretty good about our position against them. But it will be very tough for Ford to take much more market share from GM. I don't think the nation's largest company is immune, but the vulnerability of its market share in the 1980s may prove to have been a one-time opportunity for Ford.

Every manager, from the CEO on down, should be encouraging people to take bold actions and to search continuously for new ideas. You have to fight against bureaucracy and against everyone's natural resistance to change. People tend to feel more comfortable if they stick with the status quo. They say they like the people they're working with and they want to keep on doing what they're doing. That's why management has to look for ways to hold on to a sense of dynamism and energy. Without that, your company will become lethargic and boring, and your striving for innovation and creativity will be an uphill climb. That sort of company won't have the guts, or the stamina, to take on the Germans and the Japanese.

What the Public Can Do

During the 1950s and 1960s, average Americans didn't worry much about the health of the economy. Few cared whether a Barbie doll was made in China or the silverware came from Taiwan. And it never really occurred to workers that their companies might not be around in a year or two. Now many U.S. companies are in trouble, and it's time for people to start paying attention to this reality.

Some people can't help but recognize it. In cities such as Detroit and Pittsburgh, and hundreds of other industrial centers, where tens of thousands of jobs have been lost to foreign auto and steel manufacturers, people are certainly aware of the steady decline of our manufacturing. These places used to be the homes of American giants in the tire, camera, TV, or component supply businesses, but not anymore. Americans who live along the country's East or West Coast, and anywhere in the Deep South, don't seem to be as aware of the erosion, because they haven't been personally harmed by what's been happening. This is especially true in Washington, D.C., a city with a huge government bureaucracy that keeps expanding so rapidly that the people there see nonstop growth. There is always more business for the lawyers, lobbyists, and legislators. If these people went to Detroit or Pittsburgh and saw the empty factories and the unemployment lines, they would be shocked.

In the Sun Belt and the West, particularly California, people are also so used to rapid growth and development that talk about plant closings and the number of people out of work doesn't really mean much to them. I doubt that the average Californian who buys a Toyota, Nissan, or Hyundai is aware that he or she is part of a stream of actions that sap the competitive strength of this country.

American business leaders and politicians have to find ways of making the general public think about competitiveness in their homes, on the job, and where they shop. The Business–Higher Education Forum, a national group made up of CEOs and university presidents, recently came up with a good idea. It is creating a citizen education campaign of television and radio advertisements and town meetings to help persuade the public to pay more attention to our economic crisis and the problems that plague our public schools. This has begun in a handful of cities and will expand nationally in late 1991 and 1992. It is the forum's hope that the campaign will help millions realize that we have to act and we have to act soon.

What can a concerned American do? I see nothing wrong with being more aware of where a product is made when you buy it. Before I purchase a product, I have a habit of looking to see which country manufactured it. After all, since this is our country and we are on the same team, American products should get a fair shake. I realize that some U.S. products don't have a terribly good reputation for quality, and in many cases they don't deserve one. But American companies, Ford included, have made some tremendous improvements over the past decade, and their products deserve a second look. If you can find American-made products that serve your purposes, give them a try.

Consumers in Japan don't hesitate to choose domestic products over imported ones. To them, their country comes first, and they know that Japanese firms must be *ichiban* (number one) for the country to prosper. Japanese children are taught to support their fellow countrymen and all things

Japanese. Americans grow up thinking that that sort of thing is not something to worry about. For several decades after World War II, we were right; it didn't matter, because we were on top of Mount Everest compared with Japan. But now it does matter, because our economic strength has diminished over the past twenty years, and Japan is now our equal.

We should also keep competitiveness at the forefront of our decision-making every time we enter the voting booth. When deciding whom to vote for, whether it's a representative, a senator, or the president, we must remember that it's important to find out where the candidates stand on economic competitiveness. Have they demonstrated real concern about helping U.S. companies compete globally? Do they have the nerve to stand up to Japan on trade matters and to look out for U.S. interests adequately at the negotiating table? If candidates knew that winning or losing depended on their positions on these issues, I feel certain that competitiveness would become a priority in this country. As long as we are dealing with other societies that are very nationalistic and that restrict the sale of American-made goods, we have to keep the health of our economy uppermost in our minds and support this country in any way we can. That responsibility lies first and foremost with government and industry, but there's no reason why all of us can't pay closer attention to competitiveness in our daily lives.

Conclusion

On May 9, 1991, Red Poling told a large gathering of share-holders at Ford's annual meeting in Dearborn, Michigan, that 250 people from all the functional areas of the company, including hourly workers, are working as a team under one roof to build a new version of the Mustang by the end of 1993. For a number of years, people outside the company had been wondering if the venerable car would be continued after nearly thirty years in the market, and the press heralded the news as the second coming of Team Taurus.

While Red was making his remarks, a group of Ford executives flown in from around the world were gathered across town in Ford's Executive Development Center for the pilot meeting of phase three of the Senior Executive Program, the participative management seminar. As I mentioned before, we rotated the executives through the seminar twice; now they're coming back for a third cycle. I knew they were meeting because I tried to reach two of the executives, and their secretaries explained that I couldn't talk to them because they were in seclusion at the center. The secretaries were sticking to a company rule that no one, including a former

CEO, can interrupt people attending these meetings.

Those two bits of news, Red's speech and the SEP III pilot meeting, reassured me that the emphasis on people, team-work, and involvement is still alive at the top of the company. I also had a chance to hear what has been happening in product development and manufacturing. I had a long talk with John Risk, the Team Taurus leader, who now works in body engineering. He told me that the spirit of teamwork is alive and well. He visits at least one plant a week, and he said that everywhere he goes, the natural way people work at Ford is now in teams, with everyone joining in.

Frankly, I admit I felt some concern when I left Ford about whether the human relations and team efforts would continue to evolve and grow, even in hard times. It appears that the concepts have worked their way into the fabric of the company. I know much work remains to be done, but the company has reached the point where it's trying some extremely in-novative things. I mentioned the Romeo engine plant, which is run entirely by teams. Ford is at the point where hourly workers from Europe fly to America to meet with their Amer-ican counterparts to discuss new equipment and share ideas about ways to improve processes such as welding body panels and painting cars. We now have Japanese engineers from Mazda and Americans from Ford developing small cars to-gether, and groups of Europeans from various countries doing the same. The day may not be far off when a multicontinental team, with members from Europe, Japan, and America, will build a true "world car" for sale in the United States, Europe, and elsewhere. The leadership of such an effort would be taken by the organization with the best available resources.

Managers from other companies and organizations con-tinue to visit Ford to hear and see what it has accomplished over the past eleven years or so. Such visits are a far cry from the early 1980s, when Ford seemed to be a prime example of how not to do things. I believe that Ford and other American companies should continue to share ideas and learn from one another, as we build on the improvements we've made and will continue to make in the future.

What Teamwork Does for a Company

If your company successfully adopts what I advocate throughout this book, from the ideas behind EI, PM, and worker empowerment to a new managerial philosophy that encourages and rewards team players, here's what will probably happen after several years of continuous and diligent improvement. Your employees will be forming teams without consciously thinking about it. Your managers will be meeting with one another regularly and continuously pulling together people from all parts of the company to brainstorm and look for better ways to do things. Higher-level managers will be pushing responsibility down to subordinates, who have taken on a more positive attitude and are highly motivated. There will be a free flow of information, and managers will spend most of their time outside their offices, encouraging everyone and trying to help people do a better job. Your natural team leaders will be stepping forward and setting an example for those who aren't quite sure what this teamwork idea is all about. And your technically knowledgeable employees will be taking more initiative to dream up exciting products and services to surprise and delight your customers. Everyone from top to bottom will be driven by one preeminent goal: improving quality.

In an important respect, the real test of whether you have made a permanent improvement occurs when your company goes through difficult times. If these ideas aren't firmly rooted and widely accepted, then they might wind up on the list of programs that are discontinued when times get tough. But if they survive, that will tell you that your organization believes that this approach is essential in helping you work your way through whatever problems you're encountering. Management and employees will trust one another more, and will work together and accept mutual sacrifices to pull the company through.

Stumbling Blocks

I'm well aware that a lot of companies will start and stumble, or wind up spinning their wheels and wondering where they might have gone wrong. If you find that you're just not getting anywhere, you might want to ask yourself a few questions.

Do your employees truly understand what you're trying to do? Do they know what employee involvement and participative management really mean? This isn't rocket science, but you have to bend over backward to explain these ideas clearly and succinctly — and do it over and over again. One of the classic errors is to assign a corporate communications officer to explain the concepts, hand out a few pamphlets, and expect people to be converts. If employees hear the ideas only once and not from their immediate supervisors, they will go back to business as usual, and your efforts to change will fail. You should explain the company's vision and your goals, as well as the philosophy behind EI and PM, through face-to-face discussions and in team meetings. Your managers then have to build on that, day in and day out, by constantly talking to people about what it is you are trying to achieve. If you're communicating effectively, every employee will know about and understand your version of Ford's mission, values, and guiding principles, and they'll know how important it is to improve quality in everything they do. If you provide all the clues, there won't be any mystery.

Are you going far enough with your teams? Some companies launch employee involvement among the workers at the hourly level and expect that once the program has started it will continue to grow and improve results. But your improvement will be limited in this case. You need to involve all your people from all functions. For example, your technical employees need to meet in teams to tackle more sophisticated problems and find ways to improve your underlying processes. The goal is to have people work as a team anytime it makes sense.

Are you following through on your training? Many companies spend the money to teach people how to use statistical process control or how to operate sophisticated machinery, then assume the training job is finished. But your workers might have trouble remembering everything the first time. Continuous retraining is vital. In the past, it may have been possible to teach your skilled tradespeople the information they needed only once. But in today's environment, the necessary skills are constantly changing as new processes and equipment are adopted. The same points apply on the management side. Managers may react favorably to the new philosophy at a seminar, but they will need reinforcement. Give your managers continuous training by arranging to have them go through two, three, or even more participative management seminars. It takes awhile to become comfortable with new ways of functioning. Without reinforcement, your managers might slip back into the old autocratic way of managing people, and everything you've gained might be lost.

If you're having problems like these or if people generally seem slow to accept the new ideas, don't get discouraged. At Ford, we overcame our share of setbacks. And when I found myself wondering if we were ever going to get anywhere, I reminded myself of something that Peter Drucker said: get a third of your people to buy in, and the rest will follow. The third who buy in will almost certainly be positively oriented and will take the initiative to change things. Of the remaining two thirds, most are probably good people who prefer to be followers, and they will follow the lead of the others. The remainder will include the negative thinkers and the bad apples. By and large, these people will be neutralized and go along. Negative thinking can only flourish in a bad environment.

In many, many cases, changing to a cooperative culture just takes time. In fact, the ultimate transformation from a top-down or autocratic organization to a team-driven dynamo will no doubt be accomplished over several generations of management. I'm hopeful that the young people are now getting comfortable with teamwork and won't dream of doing things any other way as they become the executives of their respective companies.

The National Team

In the latter chapters of this book, I've addressed some of the issues that I believe are of major importance to America's competitiveness. I genuinely believe that we have to act boldly on our own behalf if we're going to reverse an unmistakable decline in the health of our economy. But I'm fearful that the way we react to challenges that we do not perceive as crises will make this difficult to do. In the United States, we respond magnificently to an obvious crisis, which unites us in a common effort. It's remarkable what we can accomplish, for example, in a popular military war. The question facing us now is whether we can respond to an economic crisis that is less obvious but is rapidly weakening us as a nation.

As individual leaders in local settings, we have to turn our attention to all the areas within our own power and make sure we are doing everything as productively as possible, while maintaining extremely high standards in terms of quality. I hope I have convinced you that every organization should focus on the people side of the business and find ways for all its employees to work together in a spirit of trust, cooperation, and respect for the individual. It's simply impossible to measure in advance the benefits and improvements that will flow as we engage the hearts and minds of all our people in the job at hand. These ideas will help us as individuals to do our part to overcome the competitive crisis in the years ahead.

Our single greatest strength as a nation is the value we place on the freedom of the individual. This is what gives us our vitality compared with nations that exercise greater control over their citizens. If we can harness the benefits of American individualism with the power of teamwork, we will achieve remarkable improvements in our institutions and our economy. We must do this to assure the continuing greatness of this country of ours.

Appendix A
Case Studies

Ford's employee involvement program generated thousands upon thousands of improvements in the 1980s. Here are some examples of what teams of six to thirty people accomplished at assembly plants and facilities throughout the company. In each case, affected vehicles were carefully inspected before being delivered to retail customers.

At the Wixom (Michigan) assembly plant:

In 1987, the thirteen members of the headlamp team began to look for ways to improve the process used to manufacture automotive headlamps and reduce the number of repairs made under Ford's warranty program. One concern was that the headlamps were sometimes incorrectly aimed. The team surveyed internal customers at the assembly plants to come up with suggestions that would simplify the process of making the lamps and aiming the lenses. They also talked extensively with suppliers, including Hopkins Manufacturing, which makes some of the headlamp gear. The team determined that the company should switch from the traditional mechanical method of aiming the lens to a sophisticated technology called photometrics, which uses computer-controlled screwdrivers to point the headlamp in the proper direction. Thanks to photo-metrics, the number of headlamp adjustments made under warranty dropped more than 75 percent in just two years.

At the Wayne (Michigan) assembly plant:

In June 1989, a team of nineteen people from several departments started studying ways to improve the test for water leaks in the Ford Escorts being produced at the plant. At the time, the approach was to do a twenty-minute soak test in the shipping area to expose leaks, and employees wound up doing a lot of day-to-day repairs in a highly random fashion. The team members agreed that they should switch to a process that emphasized prevention instead of inspection and repairs. The responsibility for preventing leaks was turned over to the individual departments, such as the paint shop and the body shop. Each of those areas developed their own tests to pinpoint the source of any leaks. The plantwide water-leak team used statistical process control to measure the entire process, and they reported the results to the individual departments. In just one year, the number of water leaks dropped by more than 40 percent, and the number of vehicles that passed the twenty-minute soak test the first time soared from 40 percent to nearly 80 percent. After these successes were achieved, the water-leak team presented its findings to all the local and regional plant managers. In 1990, the same water-leak control process was implemented at all the company's assembly plants. Members of the water-leak team visited all the plants to help put the new process in place.

At the Twin Cities (Minnesota) truck plant:

A group of employees in the plant's paint area formed a dirt-in-paint team in mid-1988. The team included hourly maintenance workers, outside suppliers, and a couple of salaried supervisors. When the team was formed, quality surveys showed that more than 6 percent of the trucks produced at the plant were affected by dirt in their paint. The team studied the quality surveys in depth and used statistics to isolate the source of the dirt wherever possible. In late 1989, the team invited the supplier that provided the company with air filters to join the team as an active member, and he provided the expertise to rid the air in the plant of dust and dirt that might contaminate the paint. The team also decided to buy new tools and equipment, including a laser dirt counter that identifies the location and sources of dirt and a hardened steel wedge to remove dirt without creating sanding dust. They also purchased a humidifier system to clean the air and Kanibo sponges to swab the vehicle bodies. By June 1990, the percentage of trucks with dirty paint dropped to less than one percent; the number of trucks with defects related to dirt in the paint plummeted by 76 percent in two years.

At the St. Louis (Missouri) assembly plant:

Six people — three from material handling and three from exhaust system design — formed the light truck exhaust material handling team in 1989. Their goal was to develop a "comparable to Japanese" muffler shipping rack that would deliver an Aerostar muffler from the supplier to the assembly plant with no damage during shipment, at the lowest possible cost. The team conducted brainstorming sessions and came up with a reusable shipping rack that kept the mufflers from banging into one another and eliminated the need for five million pounds of throwaway cardboard boxes, which cost the company more than $735,000 a year. In just a year, repairs due to muffler shipment damage dropped by more than 33 percent.

Multiplant or multidivision teams:

In April 1988, the company asked twenty-two employees and suppliers to form a team to improve the remote fuel door system. At the time, the company was increasingly concerned over problems with the inside switch that opens the exterior door to the gasoline tank. The team members — including senior engineers from suppliers Lectron Products, Inc., and Acco Babcock Industries, and Ford engineers from assembly plants in St. Louis, Atlanta, and Lorain, Ohio — ran numerous inspections, studied quality reports and warranty claims, and charted all the statistics on what was going wrong. They also visited several assembly plants to see where the problems most frequently occurred. After-hour meetings were held daily with employee focus groups to determine the root causes. Eventually, the team determined that the primary causes of fuel door failures lay in the design, manufacturing, and assembly of the various components. The team came up with design changes and process improvements, finding ways to reduce in-plant adjustments to the fuel door system from three to one and redesigning some components using sophisticated geometric modeling. The suppliers agreed to eliminate variation in their processes and to monitor quality closely. Thanks to the suppliers, the cost of the fuel door system has dropped by $0.53 on the Ford Aerostar and by $1.30 per unit on the Taurus and Mercury Sable. The number of fuel door problems has dropped by 91 percent.

A group of twenty-five people formed the speedometer quality improvement team in February 1988. This team evolved into a group whose members came from several divisions, including electronics and light truck. Its objective was to achieve an immediate improvement in the speedometer system. Team members studied common problems, such as speedometers that stuck on zero, trip odometers that stuck, and speedometers that wavered. They looked for the root causes of these difficulties, and talked directly to customers to find out when they most often occurred. They solved some of the problems by redesigning the parts and equipment used to make the speedometers. For example, the team came up with a longer speedometer cable, which reduced the chance of a broken cable, and it also designed a kink-resistant cable for all the cars. Teamwork was the key to resolving many of the problems. Often one team member would uncover a difficulty, another identify the cause, and a third propose a resolution. Since 1988, concerns about speedometers have plunged by 48 percent; warranty repairs have dropped 33 percent.

One of the largest teams to tackle a tough challenge was the Lincoln Town Car sheet metal team, formed in February 1988. The team's objective was to improve the quality of the sheet metal used to build the Town Car's body. That task was thought to be particularly difficult because the most important people involved are on three continents: design at the international automotive design center in England, die and assembly tooling in Japan, and manufacturing at Ogihara America Corporation in the United States. The team of thirty people included representatives from each functional area as well as internal customers from the Wixom assembly plant and body and chassis engineering. The team came up with quantifiable quality levels that must be achieved at each step in the process, even before the tools needed to cut and form the sheet metal are designed and shipped. The tool suppliers were encouraged to work with designs that would prevent problems down the road, and the team members shared ideas to support their efforts. The team designed new tools and established a quality improvement matrix that helps to identify the causes of defects and guides workers through a "plan-do-check-act" cycle of continuous improvement. The team's handiwork resulted in the highest-quality prototypes in the company's history, in terms of the quality of the sheet metal and its adherence to specifications.

At the Indianapolis transmission and chassis plant:

The power steering pump quality team, which was formed in 1985, included twenty-five members from maintenance, pump operations, quality control, and the shop floor. Its objective was to share the expertise of each member to come up with a power-steering pump that would be one of the world's best. The pump team focused on fixing major problems that could lead to problems in the final product. They devised a new lapping process, which reduced noise levels generated by the pumps by 22 percent. By switching from inspections to "find and fix" prevention, the team has enabled Indianapolis to come up with sixty-seven product and manufacturing improvements in the pump-making process, and has slashed pump production costs by $94,712 per year. As a result, the pumps made at Indianapolis were the first products at the plant to achieve Q1-level quality.

At the company's engine division:

In 1988, a team of fourteen people in the division, including purchasing managers, engineers, and designers, set out to find ways to help suppliers of front-end accessories ship their components on time and with no defects at all. The team used new-vehicle quality surveys and warranty reports to analyze problems related to brackets, pulleys, tensioners, and belts that had been purchased from fifty-six different Ford suppliers. Team members agreed to reduce the number of suppliers from fifty-six to just eighteen and to help those eighteen teach their workers statistical process control and revise their designs to improve quality and performance. These efforts resulted in a 70 percent reduction in warranty claims related to the suppliers' parts in just two years.

At body and chassis engineering:

In September 1989, a team of fifteen experts from body and chassis engineering and various suppliers, including four tire companies, set out to study the damage caused by paint repair ovens, which are used to repair chips and scratches that occur during the assembly process. The team analyzed the repair rates on 240,000 1989 model year vehicles built at the Louisville, Kentucky, assembly plant, and determined that oven-processed vehicles had to be repaired nearly twice as often as vehicles that were never put into the paint ovens. The damage occurs when the fully trimmed cars and trucks are exposed to temperatures exceeding 240 degrees Fahrenheit. The team found out that the ovens cause excessive vibrations and can even cause tires to ride poorly and wear out quickly. After doing research to determine what caused seemingly random problems throughout the company's car and truck lines, the team came up with ways to prevent use of the ovens whenever possible by eliminating the sources of chips, scratches, and other defects.

At climate control systems:

A total of twenty-three people joined the Econoline climate control systems team in 1988 to study leaks and air-flow problems related to automotive heaters and defrosters. The team examined complaints from Canadian customers about the performance of the equipment during extremely cold weather and talked extensively with hourly assembly workers, floor supervisors, and molding and product engineers at the Lorain assembly plant. They primarily looked for ways to shift from finding air leaks and fixing them with foam to preventing leaks by redesigning the dashboard area. Through the team's efforts, the number of problems with climate control systems dropped by 62 percent in 1990.

At Ford Credit:

A team of sixteen people launched the Ford Credit Customer Service Center, a pilot project created in 1988 and designed to improve the way people in that financial operation serve customers. The CSC team listened to what customers said in surveys and set up the center to respond quickly and efficiently to their needs. Risk-taking was encouraged by the team, and feedback sessions were held continuously. The team members convinced outside vendors to modify their equipment and computer software to meet the center's needs, and many team members worked irregular shifts and unscheduled overtime to put the new systems in place. The result is that the number of customers who were completely satisfied with the actions taken by the CSC passed 70 percent, as compared with 40 percent at existing service centers. The average number of customer calls needed to resolve a problem dropped from 2.6 to 1.05

at the pilot center. Based on the success of the pilot, Ford Credit is expanding the approach used there to all its operations.

At the National Dealer Council:

The car and truck dealers who belong to this council agreed that one priority should be improving the process of ordering and installing signs at Ford dealerships. A few years ago, it took approximately six months for a sign to be installed after an order was placed, and often the sign was not available until well after the opening of the dealership. Many departments — accounting, marketing, legal, systems, and the sign vendors — were involved in this cumbersome and complex process, and only 6 percent of sign orders went through correctly the first time. But then a team of dealers, with the company's support, found ways to eliminate a lot of steps in the process and open the lines of communication among everyone involved. The time for processing a sign order within the company was reduced from 109 days to 15 days, and will be slashed to 2 days when the project is completed. And 99 percent of the orders will go through correctly the first time.

At construction sites:

Both the company and its outside vendors were dissatisfied with how long it took to resolve disagreements about payments on construction contracts. Vendors wanted their money sooner, and the company wanted to avoid the administrative costs of tying the paperwork up in accounts payable. It took an average of seven months to resolve unpaid bills. Underlying the problem was a lack of trust between the two sides: the company's management believed that the vendors were trying to get as much money as they could, and the vendors thought that the company was trying to avoid paying what it owed them. Then a team of people from both sides, plus architects and other interested parties, launched a process improvement study. They managed to break down some of the stereotypes and communication barriers and began to ease the confrontational nature of quoting prices and resolving disputes. The team members agreed to share more information up front and to arrive at a cost analysis system that was mutually acceptable. The time required to settle a bill dropped from 220 days to 22 days, and the number of steps in the process fell from 87 to 43.

At the fuel-handling operation:

In the 1988 model year, several divisions were concerned about improving the accuracy of the dashboard's fuel indicator gauge. They formed a multidivisional team of sixteen experts — design engineers, product engineers, computer programmers, and outside consultants — to study ways to improve a fuel indicator system that was based on a thirty-year-old design standard. The team decided to use a fiber-optic videocamera to analyze all the components of the fuel system and to compare the fuel level inside the gas tank with what was displayed on the fuel gauge. This approach quickly determined where errors occurred, and the team went on to solve the most common problems. Two members of the team were assigned to each vehicle line. In just one year, the accuracy of the fuel indicators in passenger cars improved by 48 percent and in light trucks by 27 percent.

At the Tulsa glass plant:

A task force of twenty-five, including tin bath operators and supervisors, used a team approach to reduce variations in the thickness of car and truck windshield glass. First the team convinced management to shift responsibility for controlling glass thickness directly to the people who run the baths that produce the glass. There, hourly employees helped the team members come up with a totally different process, which involved moving the location of the first glass stretching machine, a decision that resulted in much flatter glass and more consistent results. The team devised new statistical process control charts to monitor things, and hourly members visited other plants to present and exchange ideas. By improving the process, the team reduced the amount of wasted glass, and that resulted in a savings of $24,000 a month. Furthermore, the time needed to switch from making one thickness of glass to another dropped by 50 percent, to just fifteen minutes.

At the modified vehicle operation:

Every year more than 250,000 Ford trucks and chassis are modified by other companies to create ambulances, buses, motor homes, and other specialty vehicles. In the past, Ford provided assistance to the customers for these vehicles by giving them a "body builder layout book" and offering a "body builder advisory service." But when Ford examined some ambulances in 1987, it determined that the builders were not always following the company's recommendations and that this sometimes resulted in some quality problems. That's when the company formed the qualified vehicle modifier program team to work with these customers. To be a successful supplier, Ford had to improve its understanding of these builders, their processes, and how the vehicles would be used. Every known builder was identified and visited by one of the nineteen members of the team. The top request from the builders was for better communications with Ford and better engineering support. After the visits, the team created an engineering section specifically to interact with the builders, and began publishing a monthly bulletin and conducting seminars to improve communications. In an effort to improve the design-and-build process, Ford now visits the participating customers to assess their capabilities and to offer advice on improving the vehicles' safety and quality. The team is using what it has learned to serve these customers better, and many of them are now part of the Ford team. In fact, forty-four of the forty-eight ambulance builders have volunteered to participate in team meetings and other activities.

At the (Louisville) Kentucky truck plant:

The Kentucky truck quality team was created in 1986 to improve the quality of parts coming from the nearby Sheldon Road plant. The nine-member team, which includes process engineers as well as hourly workers, initially assigned a Sheldon Road hourly employee to work full-time at the truck plant to gather statistical information to try to determine what was basically wrong with the parts for an air-handling system supplied by Sheldon Road. Hourly workers at the two plants worked very closely together, and usually spent at least one hour a month discussing ways to improve quality. The workers found ways to eliminate redundant quality checks, saving the company more than $110,000 a year. They also reduced rework costs by $23,000 a year. The number of rejected parts from Sheldon Road dropped from 1,805 in the 1986 model year to only 12 in the 1989 model year.

At the Chicago stamping plant:

A team in the tool and die shop talked about the fact that their saw blades were wearing out or breaking in half much sooner than they thought they should. After investigating, they determined that the company should switch to a sturdier, more efficient blade. Because they last longer and cut more precisely, the new blades have saved the plant more than $14,000 a year, and productivity in the sawing operation has jumped by more than 800 percent.

Workers in the materials handling department looked at the packing slips that came with shipments of parts and supplies. They designed a bright orange packing slip with a sticky surface on the back, which was easier to spot and affix to a box of parts. The new envelopes also cost $15 less per 1,000 than the old version.

The people who drive the fork-lift trucks and the repairmen teamed up to ease a changeover to a new line of Clark brand fork lifts. They were responsible for a series of ideas, including lengthening the oil dipstick to prevent workers from burning their hands on the engine block and installing wider radiator plugs to make it easier to add coolant.

At the Van Dyke (Sterling Heights, Michigan) plant:

An employee involvement group responsible for repairing a part called a carrier assembly found that they were having to repair seventy-five assemblies a day at a daily cost of $108. The team examined the process the operators used to attach a gear to the assembly, and discovered that only one tiny pin was used to position the gear in its proper place. The gears were frequently misaligned and often had to be repositioned. The team solved the problem by adding more locater pins and changing the design of several tools, so the problem has completely disappeared.

At the Sandusky (Ohio) plant:

An EI team in the department that makes car starters found that something in the process they were using was damaging about 3,000 pinions a week (a pinion is a gear with a relatively small number of teeth). Through studying the process, the team found that the pinions were sometimes distorted by the way they were loaded into the furnace. The group altered this process and eliminated 95 percent of the damage.

At the Woodhaven (Michigan) stamping plant:

One of the teams that attaches car doors discussed the fact that they weren't keeping track of alterations that were commonly made during both the day and the night shift. They created a troubleshooting notebook or log and asked every worker in the department to write down any errors he spotted. This procedure helps the team to deal with problems better and also enables management to develop a more efficient process.

At the Sterling (Michigan) transmission and chassis plant:

An employee involvement team agreed that something was creating a rough surface on a component called the drive shaft slip yoke. This was not acceptable, because the yoke has to have an almost mirrorlike finish so it can slide easily. The team decided that there were several possible causes: low-quality coolant water, worn grinding wheels, the cycle time on the grinders, and the parts flow. Eventually the group proved that lengthening the cycle time on the grinders would provide the necessary finish.

At Cleveland Engine Plant No. 1:

Members of an EI team discussed the fact that some engines seemed to be leaving the plant with insufficient oil levels. The team surveyed car dealers to find out how many cars were being serviced because of low oil levels, then began to search for the source of the problem. After talking to workers throughout the plant, team members came up with several solutions. They created adjustable dipsticks that were color-coded to show the proper oil level for each type of engine being made at the plant, and they asked management to put containers of oil in all the repair and rework areas. They also posted signs reminding people to check the oil levels before any engine was shipped. Since then, warranty repairs related to oil levels have plummeted.

At Cleveland Engine Plant No. 2:

An EI team investigated the fact that they were using far too many drill bits to create holes in a car's iron casting for the oil dipstick. The group initially tried to switch from bits made of cobalt to bits made of steel, but the newer version cost twice as much. Then they discussed the problem with the people who created the casting. After making some alterations in the design, they came up with a solution that allowed them to use the less expensive bits and saved the company $20,000 to $30,000 a year.

At the San Francisco parts distribution center:

A work group in the parts procurement area wrote a letter to all Ford dealers, asking them how the parts might be packed better. Seventy-five percent of the dealers responded with suggestions, and the packers adopted many of their recommendations. The team also visited a Ford dealership to watch how parts were unpacked, and they developed several ideas that made that process easier and more efficient for all the dealers.

At the Lima (Ohio) engine plant:

A team met to discuss ways to prevent parts called bearing caps from getting mixed up or being delivered to a worker in the wrong order. For a long time, the mix-ups had been blamed on the person who handled the bearing caps, but it turned out that the system was defective. The teams talked to more than a hundred hourly and salaried workers and solved the problem by redesigning the way the bearing caps are packaged and held in place. There was not a single reject for more than six months after that change.

At the Cleveland casting plant:

Every thirty days, a plant maintenance crew was replacing the cables on the plant's heavy-duty cranes, at a cost of $465 per cable. But a team studied that procedure and determined that some perfectly fine cables were being thrown out. Now the team keeps track of the number of hours each cable has been used, and the cables are replaced much less frequently.

At the Chesterfield (Mt. Clemens, Michigan) trim plant:

Employees agreed that they had to do something to reduce the tension and fatigue that stem from sitting at a sewing machine all day. An EI team came up with a series of exercise classes that are now offered before work, at lunchtime, and in the evening. There has been a sharp reduction in absenteeism and medical leaves as well as an improvement in worker morale.

At the Michigan truck plant:

Employees in the trim department began to talk in an employee involvement meeting about the canvas gloves they wore when they were handling pieces of automotive trim. The team decided to study the benefits of those gloves compared with those of a new polyknit glove that seemed to be more comfortable and durable. As part of their study, team members issued the new gloves to several departments. Two thirds of the workers liked them better, and said they lasted considerably longer. As a result, the entire plant uses polyknit gloves, a change that saves the company as much as $38,000 per shift per year.

At the Edison (New Jersey) car plant:

An EI team in the chassis department started to talk about the inferior quality of the stuffing material in car seats. They agreed to meet with their outside vendor, a foam supplier, and tell him about the problems they had with his products. He not only listened but agreed to improve the foam in several ways.

Appendix B
Employee Involvement:
A Methodology

When teams sit down to tackle a problem, they sometimes use a process widely known as the 8Ds, or Eight Disciplines:

D1 — Use a team approach.
D2 — Describe and verify the problem.
D3 — Implement and verify interim (containment) actions.
D4 — Define and verify root causes.
D5 — Verify corrective actions.
D6 — Choose and implement permanent corrective actions.
D7 — Prevent recurrence.
D8 — Congratulate your team.

Here is a look at how a team at the Dearborn, Michigan, glass plant's lamination department used the 8D approach to solve a problem.

D1: When the team first met, its members selected a team leader for the group, a timekeeper to enforce the time limits for discussions or brainstorming sessions, and a recorder to keep a few notes.

They also chose their area manager for the auxiliary role of team champion. (The champion in this case served as a supporter and helped to knock down any barriers to the team's progress.)

$D2$: After considering more than two dozen potential projects, the team selected improving the production of safety-glass windshields as the most interesting possibility. Then they used decision-making worksheets to focus on a common source of problems, so-called sticky vinyl. A modern safety-glass windshield uses a precut sheet of thermoplastic vinyl. During the assembly process, the vinyl blanks are unloaded from pallets and inserted between bent pairs of annealed glass. Sticky vinyl won't easily separate from the stack, and that can slow or even stop windshield production. In severe cases, the vinyl fuses into a solid block and must be scrapped.

$D3$: As an interim solution, the team assigned a worker to strip and separate the pallets of vinyl manually so that production could continue uninterrupted.

$D4$: To define and identify the root cause of sticky vinyl, the team constructed a flow diagram of the entire process, and also made what is commonly called a fishbone diagram to identify potential causes. The members agreed that there were more than a dozen root causes, including defective vinyl supplies, the cutting method, the storage time, and the height of the vinyl relative to the cutting table. The team also ran numerous trials in which they produced just one type of windshield, using blanks from one line and from one batch of vinyl.

To build their knowledge, team members interviewed engineers, technicians, vinyl set-up operators, and others who worked in the plant. They also contacted glass plants in Nashville and Tulsa to see whether they were experiencing similar problems and how their procedures differed from Dearborn's, if at all. Eventually, the team determined that storage time was the most significant variable in the process. The longer the vinyl was stored in the plant, the stickier it tended to become.

$D5$: The team members agreed that the most feasible corrective action was to adopt a just-in-time cutting system that would cut only as many vinyl blanks as workers could use immediately. Unfortunately, schedule changes and leftovers would mean that some vinyl would have to be stored, particularly over weekends and holidays. To deal with that, the team turned its attention to the vinyl storage room. From talking to suppliers, team members learned that the vinyl should be stored in a humidity-controlled room at around 45 degrees Fahrenheit; however, the temperature in the storage room rarely dipped below 60 degrees, and cooling system engineers told the team that the system was already over-worked and couldn't cool the entire work area in and around the storage room as well as the room itself. During the next vacation shutdown, the team blocked all cooling vents that didn't lead to the storage room. The test worked: none of the vinyl left in the room was too sticky to work with later.

D6: As a permanent corrective action, the team developed a proposal for funding a new vinyl storage room cooling system, and management approved the plan. The savings were impressive: at about $10 per blank, vinyl is the most expensive component in a windshield. The team's work resulted in a total cost savings of $167,193 a year.

D7: To prevent a recurrence, the team checked regularly and thoroughly to make sure that sticky vinyl didn't become a problem later on.

Recommended Reading

Many ideas in this book reflect the thinking of various writers, consultants, and business leaders in America and abroad. These are some of the books that have influenced my thinking the most.

On Management

Management: Tasks, Responsibilities, Practices (New York: Harper & Row, 1974) and *Innovation & Entrepreneurship* (New York: Harper & Row, 1985), by Peter Drucker.

Peter has been America's most consistently good author on management. I've learned a lot from him by reading his books and by talking with him. As a consultant, he is able to view a company objectively and with a big-picture perspective that very few writers seem to have.

Competitive Advantage: Creating & Sustaining Superior Performance, by Michael E. Porter (New York: Free Press/Macmillan, 1985), and *The Multinational Mission: Balancing Local Demands and Global Vision*, by C. K. Prahalad and Ives L. Doz (New York: Free Press/Macmillan, 1987).

The people at Ford used both of these books to improve the Senior Executive Program, the participative management seminar for the company's highest-level managers around the world. These books can help you focus on the global economy and on what each division has to do to help the entire corporation compete against the Europeans and the Japanese.

Conceptual Blockbusting: A Guide to Better Ideas, by James L. Adams (Reading, Mass.: Addison-Wesley, 1986).

Jim's book will help any team (or any individual) free up their minds and come up with totally new ideas or approaches to solving problems. We all tend to impose more restrictions on ourselves than we realize, and Jim offers a variety of clever exercises and puzzles that will show you that the less obvious solution to a problem is often the better one.

The Deming Route to Quality & Productivity: Road Maps & Roadblocks, by William W. Scherkenbach (Washington, D.C.: Cee-Press Books, 1986).

Bill is one of Ed Deming's best-known disciples, and his book does a good job of explaining Ed's principles concisely and clearly. Bill used to work at Ford and is now a leader in General Motors' quality improvement efforts.

In Search of Excellence: Lessons from America's Best-Run Companies, by Thomas J. Peters and Robert H. Waterman, Jr. (New York: Harper & Row, 1982).

This book is ten years old, and some of the companies featured in it are going through some difficult times, but the ideas and approaches are as valuable as ever. When we began to turn things around at Ford, we talked to Tom a lot and bought numerous copies of the book. The examples here show what happens when you treat people right and constantly look for ways to serve customers better.

The Elements of Style, by William Strunk, Jr., and E. B. White (New York: Macmillan, 1979).

I don't think you can overemphasize how important it is to communicate your ideas clearly and concisely. It's sad to see how often a scientist or an engineer has an idea but can't tell others exactly what he or she means, either orally or in written form. This book shows you how to express your thoughts as simply and directly as you can. I gave away dozens of copies of the book during my career at Ford.

On Ford

The Turnaround: The New Ford Motor Company, by Robert Shook (Englewood Cliffs, N.J.: Prentice-Hall, 1990).

Bob's book, which discusses Ford's revitalization throughout the 1980s, is an in-depth look at the way Ford launched all its programs, and provides even more illustrations of what EI teams achieved. Bob also delves into the history of the company and shows how that relates to what has happened in the past decade or so. His book is one of the most accurate and complete books on Ford that I have seen.

On Japan

Trading Places: How We Allowed Japan to Take the Lead, by Clyde V. Prestowitz, Jr. (New York: Basic Books, 1988), and *Agents of Influence,* by Pat Choate (New York: Random House, 1990).

Both of these authors deserve a medal. Clyde, who is a former assistant U.S. trade negotiator, shows us how the Japanese trade representatives win victory after victory at the negotiating table. Pat describes the amazing amount of influence that Japanese lobbyists have in our political system. I'm glad they were willing to speak up about these issues and face being widely criticized as protectionists or "Japan bashers" in the media.

On Human Relationships

On Leadership, by John W. Gardner (New York: Free Press/Macmillan, 1989).

John has written some outstanding books on the human qualities of great leaders and the ways in which companies as well as individuals can reinvigorate themselves. His philosophies reflect the importance of putting people first on a company's list of priorities.

How to Win Friends and Influence People, by Dale Carnegie, revised edition (New York: Simon & Schuster, 1981).

It's not a bad idea to read or reread this old classic to remind yourself how important it is to call people by name, consider other points of view, and emphasize the positive in all your relationships.

On Education

Among Schoolchildren, by Tracy Kidder (Boston: Houghton Mifflin, 1989).

Tracy's book does a marvelous job of showing how isolated teachers are from one another as well as from their schools' management. It also illustrates the importance of parental involvement in the schools.